BULLYING

Brilliant ideas for keeping your child
safe and happy

Dr Sabina Dosani

brilliantideas

CAREFUL NOW
The ideas in this book should help you help your child resolve the difficult situations he has found himself in. However you don't have to do it all alone. If the emotional wounds are too deep psychologists and other therapists are there to help. Don't forget to inform your child's school if bullying is going on and and if things really get out of hand don't be afraid to involve the police.

Web addresses were correct jat the time of going to press; we apologise if any have changed since then. The author and publisher are not responsible for the content of these websites.

First published in 2008 by
Infinite Ideas Limited
36 St Giles
Oxford, OX1 3LD
United Kingdom
www.infideas.com

A CIP catalogue record for this book is available from the British Library

ISBN 978-1-905940-29-5

Brand and product names are trademarks or registered trademarks of their respective owners.

Designed and typeset by Baseline Arts Ltd, Oxford
Printed in India

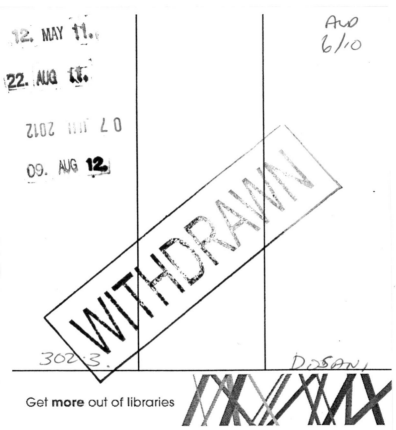

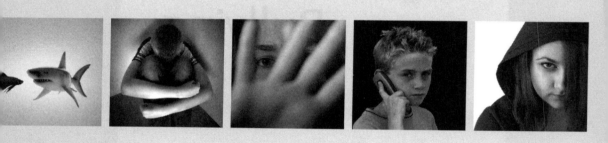

Brilliant ideas

Brilliant features

Each chapter of this book is designed to provide you with an inspirational idea that you can read quickly and put into practice straight away.

Throughout you'll find three features that will help you get right to the heart of the idea:

- *Here's an idea for you* Take it on board and give it a go – right here, right now. Get an idea of how well you're doing so far.

- *Defining idea* Words of wisdom from masters and mistresses of the art, plus some interesting hangers-on.

- *How did it go?* If at first you do succeed, try to hide your amazement. If, on the other hand, you don't, then this is where you'll find a Q and A that highlights common problems and how to get over them.

Introduction

Bullying exists. Always has done and always will. You'll find bullies everywhere: in the classroom, the playground, the school bus, changing rooms, the lunch queue – all over the place.

Bullying covers a wide range of actions, from name calling, saying or writing nasty things, leaving kids out of activities, not talking to them, threatening them, making them feel scared, taking or damaging their stuff, hitting them or making them do things they don't want to do. Some children are more at risk of being bullied, including children with learning difficulties and children who are somehow different to those around them.

In this book, I refer to various types of bullying:

- Physical, which refers to actions like hitting, kicking, taking belongings.
- Verbal, by which I mean name calling, insults, racist, sexist or homophobic comments.
- Psychological, which covers actions like spreading nasty stories and rumours, excluding and isolating, gestures and signs.
- Cyber bullying, via such things as text or computer messaging.

The most recent UK research indicates that one in four primary school children and one in ten secondary school children are bullied at least once a term. Bullying is even more widespread in inner cities.

Some people think bullying is part of growing up. That's rubbish. Children and young people have a right to feel safe and secure anywhere they go. Bullying makes kids lonely, unhappy and frightened. Many feel unsafe and think there must be something wrong with them. They lose confidence and may not want to go to school any more. It may damage their mental health and some, sadly, feel life is not worth living.

I am a consultant Child and Adolescent Psychiatrist at the Kari Centre, Auckland, New Zealand, where I help young people find solutions to a range of mental health and relationship problems. I've worked with bullied children in many settings, in the affluent and beautiful market town of Tunbridge Wells in Kent in the UK and on some of the most impoverished and violent estates in Brixton, London, to parts of the beautiful and remote east coast of New Zealand. Most importantly, I've seen first hand that being bullied is typically highly stressful for children, and for their parents who often feel hopeless and overwhelmed about dealing with it.

While everyone has always known about bullies, it is only recently that schools have started to put anti-bullying procedures in place. Ultimately bullied children and young people need to take affirmative action and this is where this book comes in. It is for everyone. Not just kids who have been bullied, but also anyone wishing to help but not knowing what to do: parents, friends, family, teachers... In these pages you will find hope and practical solutions. Mostly you will find an array of strategies that will protect bullied people.

Some ideas are aimed at younger children, some at older teenagers, some at helping adults (parents or teachers). There are many things kids can do for themselves, but also other things that they just can't implement alone. I've attempted to pitch the tone and language to the appropriate age of the person most likely to be using the idea. For instance, the research presented on the theory of home schooling is much more relevant to adults, and wouldn't work written directly for children. On the other hand, ideas like how to make friends or participate in random acts of kindness read rather clumsily when written for a parent or teacher to pass on the ideas to a child. Writing 'try to get your child/pupil/niece/whoever to do...' repeatedly became quite cumbersome. Ideas aimed at the bullied child are marked with a 🖐 symbol.

Children who call anti-bullying helplines typically do so because they haven't got an adult they feel they can confide in. My hope was that if something was written in a way that appealed to them, they might be inspired to try it. Bullying erodes children's self-esteem and I thought it would be empowering if they had some ideas that they could run with themselves, rather than relying on adults to explain and pass the information on. That said, because some decisions, like implementing a bully court, are rightly made by adults, it would have felt wrong to write the book as if all the ideas could be completed by children.

These 52 brilliant bully busters are based on UK and international research (USA, Japan, Australia, New Zealand) and best practice with what really works.

There are friends who have contributed to this book too. I'd like to thank all the children and young people in London and Auckland who have allowed me to divulge their experiences and bully-busting strategies. We agreed to keep their names and the personal details of their stories secret, but my hope is that their resourcefulness, and their bravery, will encourage you.

Mohandas K. Gandhi, who forgave his tormentors while he lay dying, said something particularly sage: 'First they ignore you, then they ridicule you, then they fight you, then you win.' Whether you've been bullied, know someone who is being bullied or are a bully yourself, I'd like to ask that you keep those words in mind. Bullies don't have to win. Just one idea in this book might be all it takes for you to follow your dreams and take on this world.

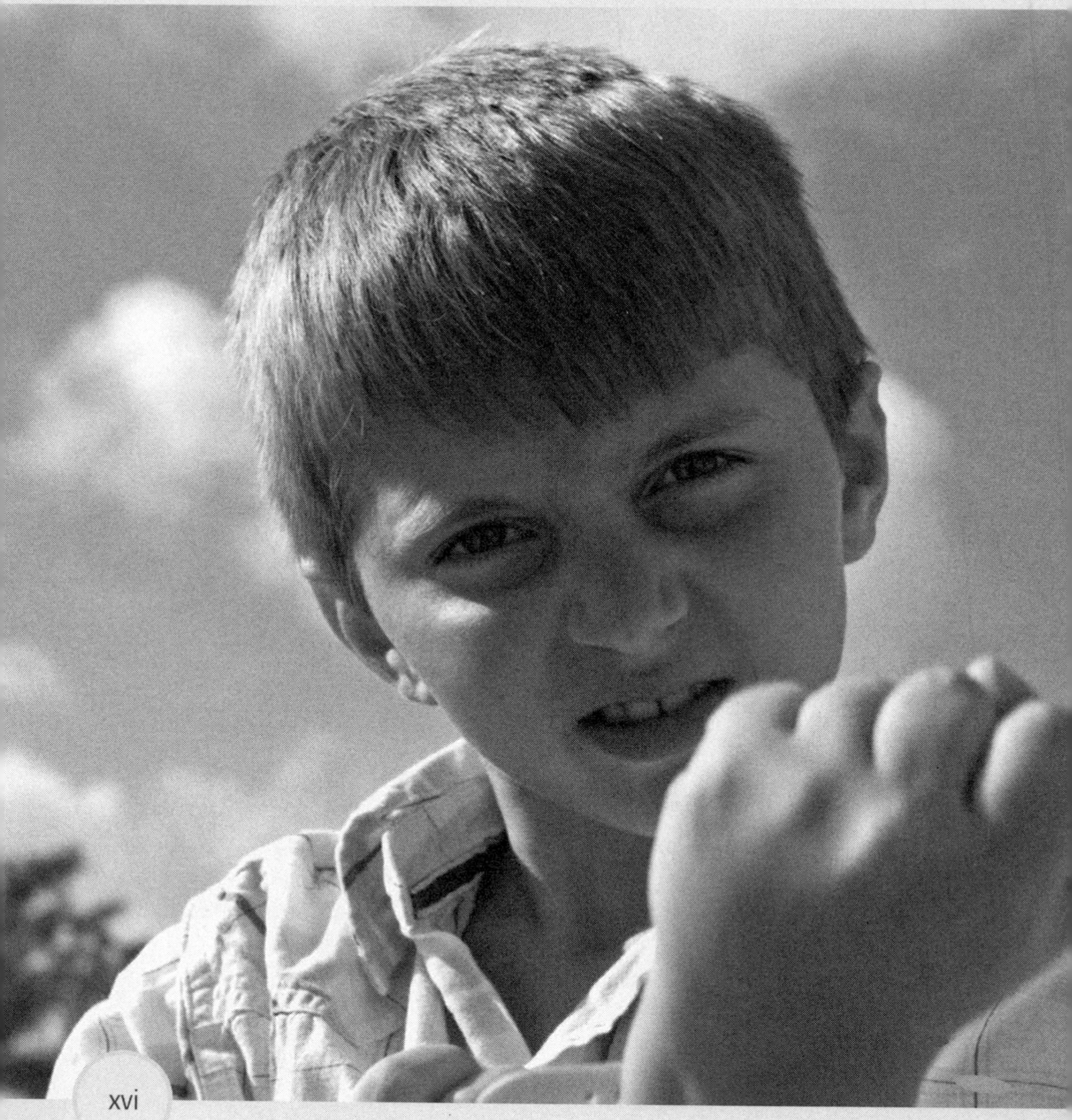

1

Bully for you

Everyone can learn to profile the common types of bully, and understanding why people bully helps with planning the response.

Learning to distinguish the types of bully — and why people bully — is an important first step.

Increasing your knowledge of why people bully will help you harness the most effective ideas for putting a stop to any bullying that's going on. Internationally acclaimed bullying expert Barbara Coloroso has developed a classification of bullies. Barbara is an educational consultant for school districts, the medical and business community, the criminal justice system and other educational associations in the United States, Canada, Europe, South America, Asia, New Zealand, Australia and Iceland. She believes there are seven main types of bullies. All these types of bullying are hurtful.

Social bully
A manipulative bully who spreads rumours, gives people the silent treatment, teases and taunts. Social bullies can pretend to be nice and can appear friendly at times, but this is most often a ploy to get what they want.

Here's an idea for you...

Next time you see or hear someone being bullied, or are bullied yourself, think about which type of bully you are dealing with, and try to identify why it might be happening. Practise categorising bullies when you come across them in books or films, too. The more you understand about different types of bullies, the better you'll be placed to develop coping strategies and fend off their attacks.

Confident bully

These are the sorts of bullies we often see on screen or in comics. Swaggering, loud, brash and with kick-ass personalities, these bullies feel good when wielding power over others.

Hyperactive bully

Hyperactive bullies are not the sharpest kids on the block. They typically struggle with schoolwork, and are not too hot at making friends, either. They often have special needs and frequently blame other people for things that are their own fault.

Fully armoured bully

Cold, callous and cruel – the hallmarks of fully armoured bullies. They can also be real charmers, but this is generally a superficial, glib charm, and not genuine warmth. Often highly determined, fully armoured bullies are quite unemotional.

Bullied bully

Bullied bullies have often been picked on by bigger kids or victimised by adults. They are usually unpopular and pick on those weaker or younger than themselves.

A bunch of bullies

A bunch of bullies is a group of kids who egg each other on. Individually they probably wouldn't dream of doing the things they do when they get together. They know what they are doing is wrong, but they do it anyway.

A gang of bullies

A gang is different to a bunch, and can be quite sinister. Gangs of bullies protect their turf or hood using violence and intimidation. They're like the worst kind of violent family.

The world breaks everyone and afterward many are strong at the broken places.
ERNEST HEMINGWAY

Defining idea...

Dr Dan Olweus is considered to be the father of bullying studies (the mother denies it). Paternity disputes aside, he has identified a number of characteristics that are common to many types of bullies. They all have a strong need to dominate and subdue other students and to get their own way, and are impulsive and easily angered. They're often defiant and aggressive toward adults, including their parents and teachers, and show little empathy toward students who are victimised. If they are male, they are physically stronger than boys in general.

How did
it go?

Q **My son is seven years old, and often comes home looking ruffled, but not obviously bruised or scratched. He doesn't say that anything is up, but doesn't seem himself and has acquired some colourful language that hasn't come from home. We haven't noticed any of his property going missing, so how else can we tell if he's being bullied?**

A *Trust your instinct. If your hunch is that there is something going on, it's worth asking him directly or asking his teacher. Bringing home swear words is not necessarily a sign of bullying, but if he is using bad language to cause hurt, it could well be. Other signs to look out for are babyish behaviour like thumb sucking or talking in a baby voice, fighting more with brothers and sisters, not wanting to see friends outside of school and grumpiness for no apparent reason. Being open and asking directly is probably your best way forward.*

Q **My son has been accused of being a bully. This really shook me up. I've been looking at the types of bully described here and can see that he might be part of a bunch of bullies, but his teacher says he has been getting into fights without apparently being egged on. I'm so worried. What can I do?**

A *I can understand you must be feeling shocked and upset. The first thing to do is make sure the teacher is right. Many kids who bully are quite placid at home, but there are some warning signs. Does he lose his temper easily? Does he get into fights at home? Has he damaged any property? I don't know how old he is, but are you worried about his use of drugs or alcohol? It's also worth remembering that sometimes teachers get it wrong, and mistake play fighting for bullying. Little boys in particular (but not exclusively) play fight. Play fighting isn't a bad thing, and helps kids learn about rules. The difference between play fighting and bullying is simple. In play fighting, both kids are in agreement about the physical rough and tumble. In bullying they are not. Keep watching for signs before jumping to any conclusions.*

2

Rhyme and reason

Poetry is a beautiful antidote to bullying. Discover how to turn your dark thoughts into lyrical couplets.

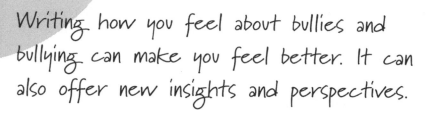
Writing how you feel about bullies and bullying can make you feel better. It can also offer new insights and perspectives.

Psychologist Dr James Pennebaker has studied writing as a form of healing for many years. The Texas-based psychologist has demonstrated many positive effects of writing to discharge negative and harmful emotions associated with past trauma. For nearly twenty years, he has been giving people an assignment: write down your deepest feelings about an emotional upheaval in your life for fifteen or twenty minutes a day for four consecutive days. Many of those who followed his simple instructions have found their immune systems strengthened. Kids have seen their grades improve.

The write stuff
A cool way of doing this is by writing an anti-bullying poem. Poetry can be a soothing remedy. Writing helps process the effects that bullying can have, and can give you a way of expressing things you'd like to say to the bullies, but can't.

Poet's corner
Try writing a poem about bullying in less than 200 words. Write the word 'bully' at the top of a sheet of paper. Now write down other words that come into your head

Here's an idea for you...

Write a poem starting each line with the word 'Someday...' and complete it with a wish you have. Why not end the poem with the word 'Someday' too? when you see that word. Think about all five senses: hearing, touch, taste, smell and sight, and add feeling. Use these words as the basis of your poem, perhaps describing your experience of being bullied, or fighting back.

As you grapple with this task, you will most likely try out different writing styles. Many people find they stumble on new ideas or discover ways of thinking they hadn't previously considered. Writing a poem about bullying can help you find ways of coping that you've never found before. Now for some tips.

Try to use metaphors in your poem. Just in case you need a refresher, a metaphor compares two objects but, unlike a simile, it does not use 'like' or 'as' or 'than'. For example: 'As I ran from the bullies, my legs were rubber.'

Many kids who do this exercise find it easier to write about themselves in the third person. This means referring to yourself as 'he' or 'she' in the poem, instead of saying 'I'. The reason people like to do this is that it helps them take an outsider's view of the bullying and they can see what happened from different perspectives. Developing this level of detachment can be healing in itself.

There are heaps of different types of poems. Your anti-bullying poem might be in one of the following forms.

Acrostic poetry is where the first letter of each line spells a word, usually using the same words as in the title. You might use the word Bully.

A ballad traditionally retells a historical event but you could tell your life story, or part of it, as a ballad.

Cinquains have five lines:
Line 1 – title (noun), one word
Line 2 – description, two words
Line 3 – action, three words
Line 4 – feeling (phrase), four words
Line 5 – title (synonym – another word that means the same – for the title), one word

Diamante is a form similar to the cinquain. The text forms the shape of a diamond:
Line 1 – noun or subject, one word
Line 2 – two adjectives that describe line 1
Line 3 – three 'ing' words that describe line 1
Line 4 – four nouns. The first two are connected with line 1, the last two are connected with line 7
Line 5 – three 'ing' words that describe line 7
Line 6 – two adjectives that describe line 7
Line 7 – noun, a synonym for the subject

People who engage in expressive writing report feeling happier and less negative. Depressive symptoms, rumination and general anxiety tend to drop in the weeks and months after writing about emotional upheavals.
DR JAMES PENNEBAKER

Defining idea...

A **haiku** is an unrhymed Japanese verse consisting of three unrhymed lines of five, seven, and five syllables or seventeen syllables in all. A haiku is usually written in the present tense.

A **limerick** is a verse of five lines, usually jokey. The last words of the first, second and fifth lines must rhyme with each other, as must the last words of the third and fourth lines. (They must not rhyme with the other three lines.)

Whatever you decide to write, don't worry too much about spelling and grammar. You can correct those later. The main thing is to have fun and be creative and expressive. In 2005, as part of anti-bullying week in the UK, a national anthology of anti-bullying poems was compiled. Many schools have incorporated the anthology into their curricula, but it might also be an idea to have local versions.

If you feel like sharing your poem with others, ask at your local library about poetry competitions. There's nothing like winning some money or seeing your work published in an anthology to give you a sense of having beaten the bullies.

How did it go?

Q **I'd like to write an anti-bullying poem but I'm not very good at making things rhyme. Can you suggest some words that rhyme with bully?**

A *I'm tempted, but instead I'll tell you that you can write a great poem without rhyme. Free verse is a type of poem that doesn't have rhyme and although it has rhythm, this doesn't have to be predictable. Put those inhibitions aside and get scribbling.*

Q **How does writing poems about the experience of bullying help people feel better?**

A *What a good question. I'm afraid that there is no simple answer. Dr Pennebaker has said that expressive writing has produced good results, but how and why it works remains a puzzle. My hunch is that it is difficult to tell because when people write, they are working on many different levels: mentally, emotionally, physically and socially.*

3

Switched on: online bullying

Being bullied in your own home is perhaps the worst kind of harassment.

Cowards hiding behind internet service providers' addresses are increasingly victimising others using email, instant messaging or by setting up malicious websites.

First-rate communication skills don't top most bullies' list of talents. So it's hardly surprising that many bullies skulk online, targeting their victims by keystroke. Cyber bullying is common; 42% of kids have been bullied online and a quarter of these kids have had this happen to them more than once. The commonest place to be bullied online is in chat rooms. Other common ways of cyber bullying are by instant message and email.

In the wake of the tragic suicide of thirteen-year-old schoolgirl Megan Meier who received intentionally hurtful messages on MySpace, many people have wondered how best to protect children from online bullying. The best idea is to establish some ground rules. Here are some basic, commonsense ones; share them with your

Here's an idea for you...

Don't reply to bullying emails. It can be very tempting, but replies will keep bullies interested in communicating. Remember, bullies want to scare, intimidate or cause misery. This is exactly why silence is such a strong weapon. Freeze them out, and they won't know if you are upset or cross.

parents to reassure them – and don't forget to use your rules when you're online.

Keep it personal

Be secretive about personal information like your name, the names of friends and family, your address, phone number, photos of yourself and your email address. Double check with an adult before posting any of this information on a website or sharing them with anyone that you only know online.

Don't always trust what people say

Sometimes grown-ups pretend to be younger online, so that they can pretend to be friends with other young people and then hurt them. Don't always trust that people online are who they say they are. It can be almost impossible to know for sure.

Count to ten

If you are feeling angry or upset, count to ten before writing a message or, even better, sleep on it. Even when you have written it, avoid sending it until you are calmer, and re-read it when you feel better. Angry messages can perpetuate bullying, and we often regret what we say in the heat of the moment.

Listen to your gut

If you have a bad feeling about a message or a person in a chat room, listen to that instinct. Those natural feelings can be a valuable guide.

From virtual to real life

If you arrange to meet someone face to face and you have only met them online previously, arrange for an adult to meet them with you on the first occasion.

If you wouldn't say it to someone's face, then don't post it online.
RONAN KEATING, Boyzone

Defining idea...

If cyber bullies have already struck, there are several things you can do:

- If you don't recognise a sender's email address or name, don't open an email on your own. Either delete it or keep it until you are with an adult, and look at it together.
- If you receive an email from someone who has bullied you before, don't open the email. Instead, drag it into a folder and get an adult to look at it for you. If it is unkind or offensive, it is a good idea for the adult to print it out and keep it as a record of what has happened.
- You can report annoying, rude or unpleasant emails to a sender's email account provider. This is usually the name behind the @ sign in the email address. And don't worry – they won't know it's you who complained!
- Most email inboxes have a filter that blocks or deletes messages from senders if you don't want any more email from them.
- Your internet service provider (ISP) can often block bullying senders too.
- Keep all bullying messages. You don't have to read them, you can just drag them into a folder, but they will help your internet service provider and the police to do something to stop the bullying.

I don't know what it is about this particular moment in human history which lends itself to the sanction of miscellaneous and casual cruelty.
JOHN PERRY BARLOW, vice-chairman of the Electronic Frontier Foundation

Defining idea...

11

How did
it go?

Q **I've been receiving nasty emails. Going by what they say, I guess they are coming from someone who knows me, but it's really hard for me to work out exactly who they are coming from, as a number of different email addresses are being used. Is there anything I can do?**

A *As you've discovered, sometimes you just can't tell who a sender is. However you can trace a sender using tracking software, which you can easily download. There are different types available, many of which are free, and the best way to find some is to do an internet search using the term 'email tracking software'.*

Q **A very malicious website has been set up about me and some other boys in my class. Other kids have posted some really horrible things about us and some are just not true. I'm upset now, but I'm also worried about the future, as once information is online, it can be hard to get rid of. I'm worried other people, say at university entrance, will see those things and that it will disadvantage me. How can I deal with it?**

A *It is very sad that some kids are victimised on websites. I suggest that in the first instance you contact your ISP. They will be able to identify who runs the site and have it removed. I also suggest you let your school know what has happened. Depending on the severity of these false accusations you may like to involve the police, and don't forget to talk to your parents. You are correct, information posted online does hang around – but if you take these steps now, you ought to be protected from adverse consequences in the future.*

4

School's out: coping with bullying to and from school

School bus bullying is increasing. It can also have serious consequences. Last year an eleven-year-old schoolboy in the UK hanged himself after being repeatedly taunted on his school bus.

When the school day starts and ends with bullying, it's almost impossible to concentrate on lessons. Nobody needs to start the day with dread. Here's what you can do.

School buses present a particular opportunity for bullies because they offer a captive audience with limited adult supervision. In some cases, bus companies are becoming more reluctant to take on school contracts or are putting up their charges. Drivers, understandably, need to keep their eyes on the road, and not the passengers, and so are often unable to intervene or stop bullying.

One day, school bus driver Ron Reynolds who had been driving for Brownsburg schools in the US for six years, 'knew something had to change'. Three young

Here's an idea for you...

If your school bus has a bullying problem, consider a 'peer bus monitor' scheme where reliable sixth formers are recruited as bus monitors to support drivers in return for free travel themselves.

people on his daily elementary school route were bullying other kids on the bus. Ron took action. He moved them up to the front of the bus, and started asking them questions. He found that by showing an interest in them, and getting to know them, their behaviour improved. 'The key is communication,' said Ron. 'When students see bus drivers not only as people, but as people who care, the behaviour starts to change.'

Not every school bus is blessed with a driver like Ron, but here are twelve ways to make the journey to school safer:

1. Consider recruiting a team of parent volunteers to act as school bus monitors. Having a second adult on the bus, who doesn't need to keep an eye on traffic, can work wonders.
2. Hold 'meet the driver' sessions before each new school year to discuss expectations.
3. Pair older students with younger students on the bus.
4. Ask the school to provide training for bus drivers to intervene and stop bullying and press for explicit procedures for drivers and other pupils to report problems.
5. Activities on the bus like music or even television programmes can divert potential bullies' attention.
6. Ensure there is a feedback system to tell drivers how any reports they have made have been resolved.
7. Encourage the kids who are being bullied to sit near the driver on school buses, or to sit by other adult passengers if it is an ordinary bus.

8. Some bus companies will agree to install video cameras to deter bullies and show who did what on the bus. This isn't always a satisfactory solution, as wily kids can intimidate others out of sight of the cameras, but they can be a deterrent.

Everyone is in awe of the lion tamer in a cage with half a dozen lions – everyone but a school bus driver.
LAWRENCE PETER, educationist

Defining idea...

9. Write to the school to make a complaint about bullying on the bus, and follow this up with a call or visit to the appropriate decision maker.
10. When it is difficult to find out what really happened, asking everyone present on the bus to write statements can be helpful.
11. Travelling on the school bus ought to be a privilege, not a right. Ask if the bullies can have their bus passes withdrawn for a week. The inconvenience to them and their parents might just lead to better behaviour.
12. Give children a whistle or attack alarm if they have to travel on public transport.

Finally, consider a walking bus scheme. A walking school bus is an enjoyable, protected and energetic way for children to travel to and from school with adult supervision. Put simply, a walking school bus is a group of children walking to school under the supervision of one or two adults. Each 'bus' walks along a set route, picking children up at designated stops and walking them to school.

Such a walking bus helps control bullying, but also has other benefits. It gives extra time for parents and reduces traffic congestion around schools (which is safer); kids are also healthier and more active. It provides an opportunity for children to interact with the road environment in a safe and active way, and has even been credited with helping to build closer communities.

How did it go?

Q **My daughter is being bullied by classmates on the way to school and on her way home, but because she isn't being bullied on school premises, her school says there isn't anything they can do to help. It's got to the stage where she is staying at home because she is so scared, and the school is now threatening to have me prosecuted for her 'truancy', which I understand they can do. Can you help?**

A *I really feel for you, but legally this is a tricky area. Some schools take the view that pupil safety is their responsibility until the children reach home, but unfortunately others don't share this view. In some cases local authorities have argued successfully in court that they are not responsible for what happens outside the school gates. My advice to you is that you ought to seek a legal opinion. Lawyers have successfully argued that it is unacceptable for a school to be able to take disciplinary and legal action against a child and the child's parents for non-attendance while it simultaneously denies responsibility for the safety of that child – especially when the child is meeting the obligation to attend the school, an obligation which has been imposed upon them.*

Q **My son walks to school as it is close by, and gets bullied on his way. Sometimes we walk with him, but we can't always do that. Is there anything else you can suggest?**

A *When kids are walking to school and being bullied on their journey, it makes sense to walk in groups and vary the route and departure times from day to day.*

5

Strip tease

Nothing brings verbal bullies into line like a bit of strip tease. Don't worry, you don't have to get any kit off, but here's how to strip the sting out of taunts.

There are several great ruses for reducing verbal bullying. This shows you precisely what to say and do.

Verbal bullying might not leave bruises or scratches, but it certainly leaves a mark. Teasing is almost too mild a term for it. Swearing, name calling, insults, threats, jokes that just aren't funny, cruel comments and harsh words are the commonest type of bullying. In many schools, experts think it's getting worse.

There are a number of different tricks you can use to stop verbal bullies in their tracks. Pick one from the suggestions below – whichever feels most comfortable and natural – and use it repeatedly. Bullies don't like to be bored, and when they see they are not getting a powerful hold over you, they'll take their taunts somewhere else. So here are those ways to strip a tease.

Say 'I want...'
Using statements that start with 'I want' are authoritative and give you back the power that a verbal bully wants to steal from you. Use a calm, clear voice, and try to look as unbothered as you can. These are some good 'I want' statements to get you started:

Here's an idea for you...

To experience greater self-confidence at stripping teases, why not get a few ready? Think of the last taunt a bully made. Which of these ruses could you have used and what might you have said? It's often easier to think of something smart to say in retrospect, so why not prepare in advance, and even jot a few down? Verbal bullies often use the same teases and insults repeatedly, so you can have a response at the tip of your tongue for the next time it occurs.

- I want you to stop taunting me.
- I want you to repeat that so that the teacher hears you.
- I want you to go away and stop harassing me.
- I want you to leave me alone.
- I want you to be friendly instead of bullying me.

Bargain

One of the good things – heck, the only good thing – about verbal bullies is that they are easier to bargain with than bullies who knock you around. It's hard to bargain when you're being held in a headlock, but if you're being taunted you can use negotiation to strip the tease of its sting.

Use 'if, then...' statements to bargain with bullies. When you are bargaining with them, think about what they want, and also what you want, and see if you can suggest a solution so you both win. For instance, 'if you leave me alone then I won't have to report you' or 'if you are going to say rude things about me, then please do so loudly so I can hear what you are saying' (and of course, so that adults can hear too).

Agreeing

Most bullies use provocative statements to get some sort of rise or reaction from you. Agreeing with them is a powerful way of turning the usual rules of bullying on their head. Your agreement will be the last thing they expect, and is a neat way to neutralise an insult. When you give one of these a go, remember that you don't have to believe what you are saying, your goal is to get rid of the bully:

- Yes, you're right, I'm a geek. I knew that already.
- Yes, I'm short. I'm also bored by you going on about it.
- Yes, I've got spots. I've also got feelings and you mentioning my spots all the time is boring.

Ask questions

Asking questions has a similar effect to agreeing, in that bullies don't expect it. I think of this response as 'one up' from agreeing, as it does require a bit of confidence, even a touch of light-hearted cockiness. Why not get your nerve up with agreeing first, then move on to asking questions? The secret with this trick is to take the bully's insult at face value, and then turn it into an innocent-sounding question, which exposes your bully's taunt for the senseless twaddle it really is. For example:

- 'When you call me dickhead, please can you explain what you mean, because I looked and I don't have a dick growing out of my head.'
- 'You keep saying I'm a lesbian, but seeing as I've kissed more boys than you, I wonder if you would explain your reasons?'
- 'When you say "fuck yourself", do you want me to do that now, in the middle of maths, or later?'

Life's challenge is to be able to look in the mirror and feel good about yourself.
ANA MATRONIC, lead singer of Scissor Sisters

Defining idea...

19

How did it go?

Q **I'd really like to try this but I'm not sure what to say to the boys who bully me. They call me a wanker. How can I turn that into a clever strip tease?**

A *These are really unpleasant but common insults. The trick with creating any strip tease is to think literally about what the bullies are saying. For example, you could try one of these alternative responses:*
Bully: You wanker.
You (agreeing): Thanks for telling me that.
You (using an 'I want' statement): I want you to stop talking about masturbation because I'm finding it boring.
You (asking a question): I'm sorry, I don't know what a wanker is. Please will you tell me what you mean?

Q **I'm worried that if I give in to the bullies, they will just carry on with worse insults. Isn't there a chance this might happen?**

A *That's always a possibility with bullies, but these techniques work because what bullies want is a response from you that shows them that they have made you sad or angry. They're not interested in clever wordplay or stimulating your curiosity, and if you agree with them in a neutral tone, there's nothing more they can say to hurt you. The chance is that they will give up at that point.*

6

Circle Time

It sounds a bit hippyish, but taking time out with a group of kids and discussing things while sitting in a circle is a successful anti-bullying measure.

Circle Time is a group activity in which people sit in a circle together to try to understand each other better and find solutions to problems.

Jenny Moseley, who is widely credited with developing and promoting Circle Time in schools, explains that it was originally developed in industry, 'to overcome the gulf that can develop between management and the shop floor. The reputation for quality which Japan enjoys can be attributed largely to the widespread use of the approach'. Circle Time also has roots in social group work and in solution-focused therapeutic approaches.

The benefits of Circle Time are that it creates a caring and respectful school ethos, enhances personal and social skills, and helps children develop their self-esteem and self-confidence. It also develops citizenship and language development, teaches democracy and problem solving, and nurtures creativity. In addition, it provides efficient and effective systems and support for all staff and creates great lunchtimes and playtimes.

Here's an idea for you...

It's possible to waste a lot of time getting a classroom ready for Circle Time. Some teachers have a circle of masking tape stuck to the floor as a quick and easy guide. Chairs or bottoms can then be placed on the circle.

Circle Time is already used regularly in many schools in the UK, Australia, New Zealand and in the US and it has an important role to play in the prevention of bullying. Using Circle Time can help young people develop skills such as listening and empathising. It can promote respect for others and individual self-esteem, is a forum within which the nature and effects of bullying can be considered and it can also be used to develop an anti-bullying code to which all members of a school community have contributed.

The Anti-Bullying Network, a Scottish support organisation, has guidelines on how to set up Circle Time. These are a combination of its guidelines and my own observations of what has worked well in schools who run successful Circle Times.

Running Circle Time

Move desks and tables out of the way and get everyone to sit in a circle. Make sure the circle is as perfect as possible, allowing everyone's face to be seen by all the other participants. The teacher is a part of the circle and sits on the same type of chair or cushion as everyone else. This helps to signal that what is happening is a special kind of classroom activity in which the teacher is a facilitator rather than a director.

An ideal number of kids is between six and eighteen; any more and conversations get unwieldy. You also need to set ground rules. I'd suggest using as few as possible, but the following three are probably essential:

■ Only one person can talk at a time
■ Nobody has to talk if they don't want to
■ Nobody is allowed to be rude or mean.

For younger children, have a talking bear. Whoever is holding the bear is the talker. When the bear gets passed on, the child holding it is the next talker (something like a cushion or a decorated piece of wood or plastic can be used instead). This talking object is passed around the circle and the only person who is allowed to talk is the one holding the talking object. This promotes taking turns and stops everyone talking at once. It also gives any shy kids a chance to participate.

Start Circle Time with a game to break the ice and encourage good listening skills. When you move on to facilitating discussion, start with a non-threatening topic, like 'My favourite place to go at the weekend is…'

Circle Time can also be used to react to a particular problem. For example, if a particular group of youngsters is involved in bullying behaviour this could be openly discussed in the circle. Another example might be if a pupil is being socially excluded because of a perceived difference; a Circle Time discussion could be initiated which focused on an individual's right to be different. This could be done in such a way that it did not draw attention to the excluded individual but promoted reflection about the underlying causes of the isolation.

Finally, always close your circle down. Devise something that signals that Circle Time is over. Some teachers use a relaxation or stretching exercise while others read a short poem.

Defining idea…

The Quality Circle Time model transforms closed, negative cultures. It is designed to help all the adults and children in schools confront bullying, disruptive behaviour and poor relationships. This programme should be at the heart of the new National Curriculum.
ANITA RODDICK

Defining idea…

I've seen the concept of Circle Time in operation in schools I've visited and been impressed by the difference it makes.
DAVID BLUNKETT, politician

How did it go?

Q **I have been running a Circle Time with a group of young teenage girls. Recently it has turned into a real 'talk and bitch' circle. How can I stop this negative, unhelpful trend?**

A *Well, Circle Time can degenerate into moaning meetings. Your task as facilitator is to keep the right tone by taking every opportunity to make positive comments. Whenever you can, make comments like 'that was very interesting' or 'thank you, that was really helpful'. If, during an open discussion, a negative comment is made, then encourage others to suggest solutions rather than just allowing them to echo the complaint. Before each Circle Time, remind yourself – and the girls – that the emphasis is on problem solving rather than going over and over the past.*

Q **The kids in my class keep breaking the rules, talking across one another and laughing at what other kids say. I remind them of the rules at the start of each session. What else can I do?**

A *If rules are continually broken during a Circle Time, finish early and ask the group for their ideas to ensure that this doesn't happen in future. Circle Time can fail, and does so for the most part when young people are still discovering what is expected of them.*

7

Bully court

It sounds like something out of *Just William* or *Lord of the Flies*, but a pupil-run bully court is a good way to give bullies fair yet firm correction.

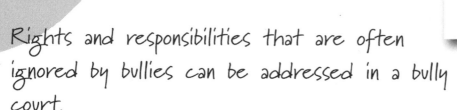

Rights and responsibilities that are often ignored by bullies can be addressed in a bully court.

The idea of school courts or tribunals goes back to the work of educational reformers such as Homer Lane, A. S. Neill, and David Wills in the 1920s.

What's more, a bully court is more than just an off-beam idea. It works. Researchers Dr Jessica Mahdavi and Professor Peter Smith from Goldsmith's College, London investigated the effects of a bully court by way of an intensive case study in one school. Questionnaires and interviews were used in conjunction with their observation of a number of bully courts and they also had access to excerpts from the school's bully court record. They found evidence of strong support for the bully court system from both staff and pupils.

Kidscape, a not-for-profit London group dedicated to child safety, has described how to set up an effective school council, which is in essence a bully court. It recommends that schools use this approach to help combat bullying. The procedure is as follows:

Here's an idea for you...

It's relatively easy to set up a bully court. You need a private meeting space, like a library, in which to meet once a week. A basic bully court typically has four pupils and a voting adult adviser. Two pupils are elected, two are appointed by teachers (to prevent bullies from packing the court). Usually, the four young judges read accounts of the incident, one version from the alleged bully, another from the victim. Then they hold a confidential hearing to elicit details from every child involved. A punishment fitting the crime is meted out to those found guilty.

1. Discuss acceptable behaviour with students and agree certain basic guidelines – the 'school rules'.
2. Sign an individual contract with each student based on the agreed guidelines.
3. Post the guidelines on bulletin boards throughout the school and in each classroom.
4. Call a school assembly and let the students explain the guidelines – involve all the staff, including playground supervisors, dinner ladies, etc.
5. As part of the guidelines, set up a student council to rule on infractions.
6. This council could comprise four students: two elected by the student body and two appointed (as an honour) by the staff.
7. One member of staff should attend the council.
8. The term of office for those serving at the council might vary but one school term is suggested.
9. Unless there was an emergency, the council should convene once a week at a set time.
10. The council would be responsible for most infractions of the rules, unless they were serious enough to involve the police, or there were family problems which made public discussion inappropriate.
11. Solutions and/or penalties would be binding on all parties, with the right of appeal.

12. The conclusions reached by the council would be written down and filed, with copies of the report going to all concerned parties.
13. School governors and parents would all receive information about the agreed guidelines and about the council, and would be invited to a council to see a mock session and to discuss the issues raised.
14. The effectiveness of the council would be evaluated periodically by students, parents and staff.

Pupils who feel they have been bullied may bring their cases to a council/bully court's attention by filling in a form and putting it in a designated bully box, telling their class representative who then discusses the case with the court, or by telling any member of staff who does the same.

Punishments for convicted bullies vary. Bully courts can't exclude anyone from school, but they could order an offender to stay after school each day for a few weeks or to eat lunch in a supervised setting away from other children. One court devised what it called 'the long and tedious punishment' – making a bully repeatedly tear up waste paper and then pick up all the pieces.

We hold a big meeting once a week and hear complaints and grumbles, and if anyone has been behaving badly we fine them. The head teachers come to the meeting too, of course, but they don't decide anything much. They trust us to decide for ourselves. Any bullying, unkindness, untruthfulness or disobedience may be brought before the meeting, and we will decide what punishment shall be given.
ENID BLYTON, from her 1940 novel *The Naughtiest Girl in the School*

Defining idea...

How did it go?

Q **Isn't a bully court just a way of bullying bullies?**

A *Viewed one way, it could be, especially if used in isolation. Bully courts work when they are part of a whole school package of anti-bullying interventions, rather than in isolation. They work especially well with peer mentoring programmes. The CEO of Kidscape, Michelle Elliott OBE, is also keen to stress they are not a universal panacea, especially if criminal assault is involved or if an offender's actions stem from serious abuse at home.*

Q **I'm a deputy head and am interested in this idea. I'd very much like to set up a bully court but there has been some opposition from several parents. Some are parents of known bullies, but others are not. How should we proceed?**

A *Parents are often concerned about the idea of a bully court. One case study showed that when parents who had reservations were invited to sit in on a court, their reservations usually turned into support. I strongly recommend you invite any concerned parents to see a bully court in action.*

8

Telling tales

If you're being bullied, it's important not to attempt to deal with it alone. But telling a caring teacher, parent, relative or friend is often easier said than done.

Why risk telling an adult if it could make bullying worse? Discover who to confide in and how to ask them to help.

Big hype surrounds telling adults about bullying. Most anti-bullying campaigns are designed and championed by adults, who urge kids not to suffer in silence and to ask for help. It's common to avoid telling adults about bullying and just hope that it will go away on its own or just stop, but sadly most bullying doesn't just stop, it gets worse until someone does something about it. Just like bullying can shatter your life, telling an adult about bullying can transform it for the better.

But many children worry that telling tales or grassing on their bullies could make what they're going through worse. Lots of kids are told to avoid tattling, so telling an adult about a bully seems wrong. It's worth revisiting the difference between tattling and reporting. Tattling is telling an adult about another kid's actions with the one and only aim of getting that child into trouble. Reporting is telling an adult about another child's actions in order to get help with difficult circumstances. You are *tattling* if you tell on someone to get that person into trouble. You are *reporting* if you are telling on someone to keep someone (including yourself) out of trouble.

Here's an idea for you...

When you are talking to an adult about bullying, have this information ready: what happened, how often it happened, who was involved, who else was there (either as bystanders or actually encouraging the bullies), where it happened and what you have done about it.

That said, it's a fact that some interventions from adults make bullying worse. So what's a kid to do?

The first step is to identify as many adults as you can who you could tell. Don't dismiss anyone outright, scribble them all down. Your list might look something like this:

- Mum or Dad
- Grandparent
- Aunt
- Uncle
- Choirmaster
- Sunday school teacher
- Teacher
- Classroom assistant

- Lollipop lady
- School bus driver
- Caretaker
- Dinner lady
- Mealtime monitor
- Tuck shop helper
- Swimming teacher

Next make a list of the advantages of telling each person. For example, the advantages of telling a form teacher could be:
- Protection in class;
- Making things better in school;
- Might halt the bullying;
- May be less likely to get into trouble for fighting back with a bully;
- Feeling a sense of relief;
- Feeling less alone;
- Feeling safer.

Do this exercise for each person on your list. When you have identified advantages, make a list of the risks that may arise from telling each person. For example, the risks of telling teachers:

- They might not keep it secret.
- They might be too strict.
- They might do nothing.
- Bullying might get worse.
- There might be nothing they can do.

Or the risks of telling your parents:

- They might overreact and call the bully's parents.
- They might not believe it.
- You might be embarrassed about feeling weak.
- You could be worried about making it worse.
- It could cause extra stress at home.

Once you have worked through this exercise and made a list of the pros and cons of telling each adult, you'll have a clearer idea of who you can tell and feel good about confiding in.

You may find that you are spoilt for choice when selecting a teacher to approach and it can often seem easier to tell a gentler, less strict teacher. However, it's worth noting that research has shown that other bullied kids have found that strict teachers were noticeably better at listening to them. They were also more geared up to take bullied pupils seriously and were ready to take appropriate action (but not without the consent of the victim), and to be 'firm but fair'.

Not to expose your true feelings to an adult seems to be instinctive from the age of seven or eight onwards. Even the affection that one feels for a child, the desire to protect and cherish it, is a cause of misunderstanding.
GEORGE ORWELL

Defining idea...

33

Whichever adult you speak to, ask them what they will do to help stop the bullying. It is important that you feel comfortable with their proposed actions. If you think their plan will make it worse, say so. There are lots of ways you could bring being bullied up with an adult. For example, you could say, 'There's something happening that's stressing me out. Please can I talk to you privately about it?' Finally, telephone helplines are a confidential source of advice. Many kids find that it is easier to express feelings to a trustworthy stranger first.

How did it go?

Q **I want to tell my head of year that I have been bullied. She's quite strict so I think she could do something about the situation I find myself in, but I'm scared of going to see her. What can I do?**

A *Seeing her sounds like a good instinct. Your head of year has probably been helping people with bullying for a few years, so is well placed to help you. Taking a friend with you is one option. Alternatively you might consider speaking to the teacher with a parent present.*

Q **I told the school dinner lady that I have been bullied and she said she would speak to my head of year. That was three weeks ago and nothing has changed. What should I do?**

A *Well done for speaking up to someone you trust. Unfortunately, you can't guarantee that the first adult you confide in will take appropriate action. When it comes down to it, the bottom line is that teachers are more likely to take action than non-teaching staff, so please tell someone else, and keep talking until something changes.*

9

Safety in numbers

You know the expression, two's company but three's a crowd? A crowd is a brilliant way of deterring bullies.

Get one step ahead of the bullies by buddying up with two pals and being inseparable at bullying hot spots.

When it comes to bullies, there really is safety in numbers. Bullies tend to pick on kids who are on their own, and avoid children in larger groups. Buddying up with two pals is a high-impact way to be liberated and safe. Staying within arm's length of two good friends during risky times during the school day and in bullying hot spots is a powerful way to ward off trouble.

In his book *Vital Friends* Tom Rath has described a number of different types of friends:

Builders motivate you, help you see your strengths and advise you on how best to use them, and are generous with their time.

Champions stand up for you and your beliefs, and they praise you to everyone else they know.

Collaborators are friends with similar interests, those with whom you are most likely to spend your time.

Connectors get to know you and then instantly work to connect you with others who will share your interests or goals.

Here's an idea for you...

Being seen with others conveys popularity and confidence. Bullies find both these traits repellent. When thinking of your trio, choose people who share your interests and share at least some of your most important values. It's always a good idea to hang out with people who are willing to stand up for what they believe. It's harder to be bullied with friends like this.

Energisers are fun, cheer you up when you're down and are always available to boost your spirits.

Mind-openers stretch your viewpoint and introduce you to new ideas, opportunities and culture.

Navigators are the ones you seek out when you need guidance and counsel; they're great at talking through your options.

Companions are the first friends you call, with good news or bad. They are always there for you.

Two champion or companion friends to keep close are worth their weight in gold. You probably hang out with friends a lot already, but there are some key times you ought to be in your trio:

- At play. Playgrounds, football pitches and the like are the ideal places to try out your trio technique. Bullies are much more interested in targeting kids who are on their own, so are likely to leave your team alone. If you see someone who hasn't got anyone to talk to, invite them to join you.
- On the way to school. You don't need me to tell you that bullies often strike on the way to and from school. Even if you are usually bullied in school, it's worth keeping two friends close by on your journey when you start sticking together, as bullies may be on higher alert for opportunities to get hold of you alone. By pre-empting them, you ensure your safety.
- In corridors. School corridors (think indoor playgrounds) are another bullying hot spot. Traversing vast corridors alone is a no-no.
- At the bus stop. A group of kids chatting or playing a game at a bus stop is a lot safer than one kid looking nervous alone. If you don't go the same way home as

your in-school trio, it's time to find some bus-stop mates, but there may be times when there are no kids to talk to. While you are likely to have been told never to talk to strangers, there may be some times when you feel you must – if you feel you are being threatened, for instance. Discuss this with your parents, but someone like an elderly lady or a young mum may be a good bet. Alternatively, get an adult to collect you. It might feel embarrassing, but it's better to be blushing than bullied.

Hold a true friend with both your hands.
Nigerian proverb

Defining idea...

- At the skate park, or the swimming pool, or the ice rink, or anywhere else you hang out without adults.
- In the toilet (and before you say, 'uggh, gross', I don't mean in the cubicle). Keep in mind that kids who go to the toilet in a trio rather than individually are much more likely to be left alone by bullies.

How did it go?

Q **I feel embarrassed and like bullying is my problem so I don't want to drag my friends into it. I'm worried they might get picked on too. Any ideas?**

A *Why not talk to them about it? Chances are they will want to look out for you and make sure you are safe. That's what real friends do, and I'm sure you'd do the same for them. I can understand that you don't want them to get picked on. Firstly, that's more likely to happen if you go around in a pair, instead of in a trio. Secondly, talk to your friends about talking to a teacher or parent as well as hanging out together, to reduce the chances of all of you being victimised.*

Q **I've been picked on a couple of times, even though I've had my friends with me. They didn't know what to do, so did nothing because they were scared of making it worse. They asked me what they can do to help me if it happens again. Any advice?**

A *What a shame that some bullies get pleasure from an audience. It sounds as if by being quiet bystanders, your friends have unintentionally encouraged further bullying. But there is a lot they can do. For instance, verbally showing disapproval by saying something like 'that's not OK', getting help immediately from a teacher, or getting a larger group of friends together to protect you are all good steps. They need to stand up for you and actively protect you. Ask them to write down what was said and done and the names of everyone who witnessed it and give this to a teacher. This will show the bullies that your trio means business.*

10
Changing schools

If bullying persists, despite the school's involvement, moving schools may be the best way of moving on from bullies.

Changing schools seems like a last resort, but sometimes making a fresh start is the best option.

When kids are averse to going back to school because of bullying, it sometimes makes sense to start afresh. Before you move schools, it's worth knowing what a move in school can help kids achieve and what it can't.

It may be unrealistic to expect a child to feel better straight away in a new school. Bullying often leaves emotional hurts and scars, and sometimes these hurts come to the surface in a safer environment, like a new school. Changing schools in itself won't make anyone feel more confident, bump up battered self-esteem or make them look like Elle McPherson. There's also no cast-iron guarantee that bullying won't happen in a new school. All that said, many kids are desperate for a new start and, for many, a change in school helps them move away from being bullied and allows them to get on with learning and making friends.

New schools come with an assortment of people who are – in theory – all potential new friends. It's easier for children to walk into a class of relative strangers if they've already put a couple of faces and personalities to the names. In many cases it is possible to visit a school in advance, perhaps for a fun lesson like art or sports, so investigate this. Going to something like that will give your child a chance to meet people first, so it isn't too daunting on day one.

Moving from one school to another often causes emotional and scholastic stresses. If you or your child find changing schools too dizzying to contemplate, don't be disheartened. It's a big step to consider moving to a new school.

Before you commit to a change of school, consider four things:

- Can you think of any other way to resolve the bullying that doesn't involve moving?
- Does the new school have a comparable curriculum?
- How will your kid stay in touch with established friends?
- Do the bullies have friends or gang members in the new school?

When you're looking at possible schools, obviously academic and social factors will be on your list. But it's also worth checking out the school's anti-bullying policy. If you can, move kids to schools where they already know a couple of others.

Decide on the 'line'

If a child starts a new school, especially part way through the school year, people are going to ask why. It's best to be prepared for this by having an answer ready, so talk it through. It doesn't have to be the truth, although before your son or daughter makes up an elaborate tale of having been shipwrecked and adopted by pirates who have moved into the area, it's worth remembering that the truth has a way of coming out. Especially at school fundraisers and socials. The following lines have all been used to good effect:

- 'My parents felt my old school didn't really meet all my needs.'
- 'I found it hard to find people to get on with at my old school.'
- 'I heard good things about this school and wanted to join it.'
- 'I have some friends who are at this school and I thought it would be neat to go to the same school as them.'
- 'I was bullied in my other school and wanted to make a fresh start.'

My school was so tough the school newspaper had an obituary section.

NORM CROSBY, American comedian

How did it go?

Q **My son's been bullied relentlessly for the past two years. The school have done what they can, including excluding one of the ringleaders, but it hasn't stopped. It's affected his schoolwork as he's missed a lot of lessons and has found it difficult to concentrate during the ones he has been in. We've agreed that he can move to a new school, but we think it's better that he starts at the beginning of the year. He just wants to leave his old school as soon as possible. What do you think?**

A *There are two things to weigh up. The first is whether your son is able to access the curriculum at all, given the ongoing bullying. The second is whether he feels able to cope with potentially attracting attention by being a newcomer part way through the school year. It can be easier to blend in when you join at the start of a school year, but it might be that he feels the bullying is making him so miserable that this is a more minor consideration. Only he can really be the judge of this, but for what it's worth, if he's not getting anything out of his current school but misery, I'd move him sooner rather than later.*

Q **Our daughter's been badly bullied and wants to change school, but she's also been talking about correspondence courses a lot. She would really like to switch to one of those but we think it would be better for her to have a new start at another school instead; so do her teachers. What's your view?**

A *Correspondence courses have a lot going for them. Students can work at their own time, at their own pace, and she wouldn't be distracted by bullies either. However, she'd also have to be almost supernaturally self-motivated to finish her education entirely by correspondence. And, unfortunately, friends and fellow learners aren't easily accessible by correspondence course, either. I can understand her wish to bail out of school completely, given her bad experiences, but I'd suggest giving another bricks and mortar school a go. Many people find that bullying doesn't follow them and she might make some good friends.*

44

11

Walk tall

Over half of our communication is done with our bodies. Changing your body language can change you from would-be victim to someone bullies will walk away from.

Discover why walking tall with your head held high and shoulders thrust back is less likely to make you a target for bullies.

Ever wondered why bad guys often hide behind sunglasses, under or caps hoodies? When we communicate, only 7% of what we're saying is interpreted from the words we use. A further 38% is picked up from our voice. This includes the speed we speak at, and also tone, pitch and rhythm. A whopping 55% of our message comes across through body language.

Looking anxious, scared or intimidated will show itself in your body language. Here's a secret. Bullies find it hard to pick on kids who walk tall and look confident. They would much rather pick on a kid who looks intimidated. Many people who have been bullied or picked on have a tendency to walk small, hunching themselves up, which has the effect of encouraging bullies even more.

Many kids spend a lot of time worrying about what to say to bullies, and don't focus enough on what their bodies are saying. Your body language tells bullies heaps about you. Walking tall, with a straight back and brisk pace, exudes confidence.

Here's an idea for you...

Practise confident body language in front of a full length mirror. Aim to stand with your head up, shoulders back and relaxed, breathing deeply – and then take some steps, aiming to look confident and purposeful. Pay attention to how you feel. You *might* feel like a bit of a dork doing this, but nobody will know. Seeing yourself in the mirror helps you see yourself as others see you and gives you a chance to perfect your stance before giving it your best on the streets and in the classroom. You could also try videoing yourself.

Standing with hands on hips can make you look ready for action, but can also be interpreted as an aggressive gesture. A hunched or stooping posture is often associated with a lack of confidence. It can mark you out as a good potential victim for bullies.

To avoid looking like a good target for bullies, steer clear of:

- Walking with your hands in your pockets. This makes you look dejected.
- Hunching your shoulders. This makes you look unsure.
- Playing with your hair. This tells bullies you are insecure.
- Touching your face. This can make you appear worried.
- Having your hands clasped behind your back. This can make you appear apprehensive.
- Biting your nails. This makes you appear nervous.
- Sitting with your arms crossed across your chest. This can make you appear defensive.

Instead aim to:

- Walk tall.
- Keep your back straight.
- Hold your head high.
- Sit with your hands clasped behind your head.

■ When standing still, keep your feet shoulder width apart and lean slightly forward.

All these postural tricks make you look confident, cool and poised.

Body language expert Tonya Reiman explains why it is so important to walk tall. 'When they're not feeling confident, people tend to drop their neck into their shoulders and slump down a little bit. One of the things that I tell people to do is drop their shoulders down and elongate their necks and to smile. Smiling sets off good feelings in the prefrontal cortex, so it kind of makes you feel better about life. So I tell them: make eye contact, smile, elongate your neck, and fix your posture.'

She advises people to tilt their heads when speaking with others. 'You want to lean into them a little bit, but never entering into their intimate personal space,' she says, 'because what you're trying to convey is your level of interest so that in their mind they are the only people that matter. And just that little interaction can cause them to begin to really trust you and feel rapport.'

When confronted by a bully, it can be a natural reaction to make yourself small and cower, but don't be afraid to take up some space. For example, sitting or standing with your legs apart shouts 'I'm full of self-confidence' and lets bullies know you are comfortable in your own skin.

Next time you're out, indulge in a little people watching. Start by watching the way people act and hold themselves. Look especially at people who you think of as confident and who are left alone by bullies. Why not try to copy some of their movements? If you wear sunglasses, nobody need know they are being observed.

Body language is a very powerful tool. We had body language before we had speech, and apparently 80% of what you understand in a conversation is read through the body, not the words.
DEBORAH BULL, dancer, Royal Ballet

Defining idea...

How did it go?

Q   **It feels funny when I try to walk taller. How can I make it feel more natural?**

A   *Please relax. New habits take a while to feel normal. If you've spent months or even years looking at the ground, holding your head up is going to feel a bit odd. Trying to make too many changes at once can be bewildering and feel overpowering. Try to pick one new body-language habit each week and practise it often. Even small changes can have big effects on body language and bullies, so be encouraged and don't give up.*

Q   **How can body language be used to deter bullies once they have started talking to me?**

A   *When another person – bully or not – talks, you will encourage more conversation if you nod, raise your eyebrows or show some other reaction. If you avoid these reactions altogether, you signal your disinterest. Do that. Seeing that they can't get a rise from you, they are likely to move on.*

12

Fight or flight: self-defence skills

Self-defence might sound as if I'm suggesting that you beat bullies to a pulp, but good self-defence also means doing all you can to avoid a fight, using brain before brawn.

Formal self-defence instils confidence. This is good news because feeling confident makes you less of a target for bullies.

Self-defence skills can help you (and adults, of course) decide what to do if attacked. Specialist self-defence classes also teach particular skills for breaking an attacker's grasp and ways to ensure a safe and swift getaway. One of the best things you will gain from self-defence classes is self-confidence. Having a few dry runs means that you will know what to do in the heat of the moment. Self-defence training can increase your options and help you prepare responses to slow down, de-escalate or interrupt an attack. Like any tool, the more you know about it, the more informed you are to make a decision and to use it.

People who learn self-defence are not more violent, but are better able to judge whether to use force, and what degree of force to use, if attacked. When someone is a threat to your personal safety then you have a right to use reasonable force for

Here's an idea for you...

Just as you can't learn to drive without getting behind the wheel, you can't perfect self-defence skills by reading a book. Check out your local colleges, martial arts schools and YMCAs for details of self-defence classes for young people and get started. If you go to these classes with friends, you can practise together and reinforce important lessons.

protection. The aim is always for a peaceful end to any attack, but survival skills help you reach that aim. Self-defence is a set of awareness, assertiveness and verbal confrontation skills, together with safety strategies and physical techniques, that enable someone to successfully escape, resist and survive violent attacks. A good self-defence course provides psychological awareness and verbal skills, not just physical training.

Here are ten simple self-defence tips that you can use when confronted by a bully who threatens to physically assault you.

1. If someone grabs you, make a scene. First shout out as loudly as you can. Shout something like 'back off' or 'go away'.
2. If nobody comes to help, shout 'fire' as loudly as you can. People often run out to see what is happening when they hear 'fire'.
3. Consider throwing your bag or whatever you can and scattering your belongings everywhere. This may distract the person holding you so that you may escape.
4. If you are regularly being victimised, carry a whistle in your hand or around your wrist. Use it if you feel threatened.
5. If you are being hurt, you can use reasonable force back to free yourself. Never hurt anyone more than you have to, but if you need to hurt someone in order to startle them enough to loosen their grip so you can run away, then do so.

6. If you are being held, start running as hard as you can, even if you can't get free. Move your legs as though attempting to kick yourself in the bum. If a bully is moving, he is unlikely to be protecting his groin; your heels will hurt if they make contact and this ought to startle him enough to let you go.

My other brother-in-law died. He was a karate expert, then joined the army. The first time he saluted, he killed himself.
HENNY YOUNGMAN, American comedian and violinist

Defining idea...

7. A short, sharp thump to the knees can slow your attacker down, enabling you to run away.

8. If you are being hurt, try to stomp hard on your attacker's toes. Squished toes often startle a bully, allowing you a chance to get free.

9. If you still can't get away, drop to the ground and hold onto something that makes it difficult for a bully to lift you. Select the nearest heavy or fixed object, like a rubbish bin, bicycle or railing. The following grip makes it difficult for someone to release your hold: one hand should grab and hold the underside of the other lower arm and wrist, and vice versa. While you're holding on, make as much noise as possible to attract help.

10. Finally, if you're being attacked, don't stop looking for a way to get away safely. Remember, your goal is to get away, not to hurt. As soon as you can, run to a place where there will be adults who can help you.

How did it go?

Q **I've got bad asthma which makes me vulnerable to bullies. I'd love to be able to defend myself but worry I might not be fit enough for classes. What do you suggest?**

A *Rest assured, you don't have to be totally fit to learn to defend yourself. A good instructor will be able to adapt techniques to different ages and abilities. Speak to an instructor about what you are looking for and take it from there.*

Q **My mum's worried that if I learn self-defence and use it to fight back, I'll get beaten up even more badly by the bullies because it will just make them angrier. What do you think?**

A *There's no evidence to suggest this would happen. For many kids who've been bullied, the emotional hurts linger after physical hurts have healed. I hope I've impressed on you that self-defence is about being mentally prepared and that physical force is a last resort. It is known that using self-defence doesn't increase the level of physical injury inflicted by bullies; the reason for using self-defence is to get away from serious physical attack as soon and as safely as possible. It is, of course, a no-brainer to get in a pre-emptive strike and that's not self-defence, but a good instructor will enforce that message.*

13

Run for the hills

If you run regularly, you acquire some important anti-bullying attributes.

Running is also a great way of letting off steam and burning off some of the adrenaline that bullying generates...

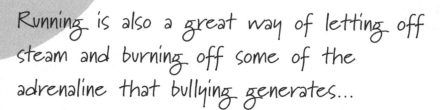

Bullying has powerful effects on the brain, but you can counteract them. A brain is essentially a colony of ten billion interconnected cells that communicate with each other. Between each cell there are spaces called synapses. A synapse is a sort of junction between two brain cells, where the end of one almost touches another. Imagine you're talking to a friend and you're both on a bus. Easy, you just turn and speak. But when you want to let another friend know that you'll be late because the bus is stuck in a jam, you use your phone.

Cells are a bit like you using your mobile phone when they communicate with each other across the synapses. Electrical charges are used to communicate inside brain cells. But electricity doesn't carry across the synapse, so brain cells release chemical communicators. These chemical communicators are usually stored in little capsules called vesicles and swim into synapses when needed, carrying their message to the next cell. You may have heard about these chemical communicators before; they're called neurotransmitters. There are many of these, and they carry different messages. Some calm their part of the brain down, while others get it all excited.

Here's an idea for you...

If you're feeling motivated to start running, the good news is that you don't need much kit. Your first stop should be a local sports shop for a good pair of lightweight running shoes. Choose a shop that will watch you running down the road or on a treadmill as they will then see exactly which type of shoes are best. You might need some lightweight cotton socks, too. You don't need designer running gear when you start out; you've probably already got comfortable shorts and tops. A cap is useful because it helps you avoid sunburn and you might like to keep it on in the winter to avoid heat loss. A water bottle is essential.

What's all this got to do with bullying? Well, I'd like you to visualise an almond. No, really. There's a part of your brain that looks like an almond. It's called the amygdala and is responsible for regulating emotion and behaviour. Anything that happens to you is filtered through this little almond; it assesses whether or not you are under threat. When your amygdala perceives that you are in danger, it puts together a chemical response. These chemicals help the rest of the brain plan how to escape from the threat.

The precise chemical configurations designed by the amygdala to deal with, say, a bully, are stored so you can respond more quickly if you encounter a similar threat at another time. The problem with this is that repeated bullying can put your brain into an almost permanent jumpy state of high alert, which is not good.

The good news, however, is that exercise also has powerful effects on the brain. Exercise increases the levels of three neurotransmitters that are necessary for emotional regulation, the ability to focus, mental alertness and calmness. If you don't have enough neurotransmitters you can suffer from depression, mood swings, irritability, anxiety, attention problems, stress and sleep problems. And that's why exercise can help you deal with the stresses that bullying can cause.

Kids who exercise regularly have improved confidence and higher self-esteem. They are much more even tempered and have fewer angry outbursts, are more optimistic all round and also develop better team-playing skills, which can be very useful.

I ran and ran every day, and I acquired a sense of determination, this sense of spirit that I would never, never, give up, no matter what else happened.
WILMA RUDOLPH, US track star

Defining idea...

You don't need me to tell you that these are exactly the sorts of attributes needed to fend off bullies. And there are other benefits, too: if you exercise regularly you're likely to be thinner (exercise helps control body fat) and are less likely to get overweight, and you have stronger muscles and bones. So get moving, in a very practical way, by starting a regular running programme – that's the simplest way to begin.

Kids who run look forward. They enjoy a constant sense of achievement and individual rather than team success. Battered self-confidence usually recovers when they see results of their personal effort. And, although in most instances it's better to walk rather than run away from bullies, being able to outrun your tormentors may just come in handy.

It's worth giving it a go. Even if you can't run between your bedroom and the bathroom, this programme will have you running a kilometre in twelve weeks. To follow it, commit to doing the prescribed exercise on every school day, and repeat it three times.

- Week 1: run for one minute, walk for two; repeat…
- Week 2: run for one minute, walk for one
- Week 3: run for two minutes, walk for one
- Week 4: run for three minutes, walk for one
- Week 5: run for four minutes, walk for one

- Week 6: run for five minutes, walk for one
- Week 7: run for six minutes, walk for one
- Week 8: run for eight minutes, walk for one
- Week 9: run for ten minutes, walk for one
- Week 10: run for ten minutes, walk for one
- Week 11: rest
- Week 12: run a kilometre without stopping.

How did it go?

Q **It's really hard to find time for exercise. School is busy, homework is demanding. I just don't see how I can fit this in. When do you suggest?**

A *According to the American Academy of Pediatrics, the average child is watching about three hours of television a day, so just work out how you are spending your time. Even if you're well below this average, bin your box (or stop playing computer games) for a while and pound those pavements.*

Q **How much exercise is enough?**

All children over two years old ideally need sixty minutes of moderate to vigorous exercise on most, preferably on all, days of the week. Aim for forty minutes per day of exercise. This might sound daunting, but you can split it into two twenty-minute sessions, or even four ten-minute ones.

14

R Time

Helping children talk and get to know one other fosters accepting attitudes and broad-mindedness.

Discover how random pairing can help prevent bullying. It's a key part of a great school programme, R Time, and has been used in the UK, Norway, Iceland and Australia.

'R Time' stands for relationships to improve education. It's a school programme, developed by Greg Sampson, a former primary school headteacher with thirty-two years' experience of working in schools located in deprived and impoverished areas. It has been designed to help children develop more positive relationships, and that can have a real impact on any bullying problem.

One key feature of R Time is a concept called random pairing. Now, I realise random pairing might sound more like the sort of idea you'd find in a relationship book but do be assured, it isn't. In this context, it means that rather than always working with their best mate or neighbour on the next desk, the children work through up to thirty different activities with lots of different children. These activities include discussions, creative tasks and problem solving, all of which help build friendships and develop citizenship skills.

Here's an idea for you...

Make a class anti-bullying quilt to exhibit to the entire school. It's a fun activity that also allows kids to develop more positive relationships while they are working on an anti-bullying project. Once children have been divided into random pairs, give each pair a felt square, 20 cm by 20 cm. Get them to decorate the felt squares with anti-bullying messages using fabric paints or stitching. Each pair should then have an opportunity to explain the message they have chosen to depict to the rest of the class. Finally, stitch the squares into a large patchwork quilt and display it somewhere where it will be seen by the whole school.

Each time an R Time session takes place, kids are randomly paired with a different partner, using pairing cards. This approach makes it possible for them to work with everyone in their class. Once they've been paired, they greet each other with an upbeat statement, like 'Hello, my name is Bruno. I'm really pleased you're my partner today, Milly'. When they have completed the activities, children give feedback on their experiences to the rest of the class. They also thank their partner and say something positive and warm to them like 'I enjoyed doing these activities with you today, Floyd'.

Researchers explored the potential benefits of R Time in 2005 in eight primary schools where over 1000 children were involved. Their study demonstrated that R Time had a positive impact on social inclusion, contentment in school, relationships and promoting a positive ethos. The students also perceived that their school was against bullying and were increasingly willing to talk about it.

One of the best things about this simple approach is that teachers can use some of the principles from R Time straight away in almost any lesson. Introduce random pairing before a class activity by distributing a pack of memory cards or snap cards, or any type of cards with identical pairs, and getting each kid to pair up with a person who has the same card as them. Bear in mind that children should introduce themselves politely at the start, and feedback their activity to the rest of the class and thank one another positively at the end.

The best way to destroy an enemy is to make him your friend.
ABRAHAM LINCOLN

Defining idea…

Here are some things to do in pairs:
- Be mirror images of each other.
- Interview each other for the news.
- Complete a jigsaw.
- Check each other's pulse.
- Decide what you would add to the school's anti-bullying policy.
- Take turns, paragraph by paragraph, to tell a story that begins with this introductory statement: 'Ursula started standing up to the bullies on Wednesday…'
- Make a collage showing three differences between you and three similarities.
- Write a poem that mentions every member of the class.
- Take turns naming animals for a letter of the alphabet; the last one to think of a word wins, and you move to the next letter.

Although it was originally developed for younger children, R Time can be used successfully right through secondary school. Random pairing could be part of the whole school ethos, in fact. You could use random pairs, for instance, in staff meetings, sports activities, parent – teacher association meetings and after-school groups. And, finally, these principles could be applied not only in tertiary education but also in life outside the classroom.

Thank you for helping the bullies in our class to not bully again.
PRIYHA, nine-year-old schoolgirl in Coventry who took part in R Time

Defining idea…

How did it go?

Q **I've approached my child's teacher and she says there's already too much on the curriculum to take on anything like this. What do you suggest?**

A If you are trying to persuade a teacher to just try R Time, why not suggest incorporating the random pairs idea into an existing lesson? Perhaps children could work on maths problems in random pairs, adhering to the positive introductions and thank yous. Many teachers find that R Time dovetails well with the rest of the curriculum, especially citizenship and personal and social development lessons. Once this teacher has seen the benefits first hand, she is likely to come on board.

Q **Can you explain what the pairs activity that is referred to as 'making mirror images' entails?**

A This is an activity in which one person copies the movements made by the other person. Mirroring another person's body movements heightens self-awareness and stimulates tolerance of differences. It also means that children have to be thoughtful about each other as they focus on making their movements attention-grabbing and slow enough for the other person to mime.

15

Stop, think, do

Traffic lights are not just for traffic. Find out how the three familiar lights can act as a prompt for a powerful technique that has helped children all over the world.

Stop, think, do. This little mantra is marvellous. Bullied kids can use it to help make good friendships and it can also help stop them from lashing out inappropriately.

The 'stop, think, do' technique was developed by child and family psychologist Lindy Petersen. I was introduced to it while running a group for children who struggled with social skills alongside a colleague in London's Brixton in a Child and Adolescent Mental Health Service. The children in the group had been exposed to diverse pressures – crime, drugs, family breakdown, abuse and neglect – but everyone in the group shared the experience of being bullied, too. They struggled to solve problems positively and make friends. When my colleague and I thought about what we would teach the group, she suggested 'stop, think, do' because it had been widely evaluated in different schools and had shown brilliant results.

I've since shared the idea with many children who have been bullied, on both sides of the world. Kids who've been bullied often have difficulty with what we call 'social skills'. That sounds like an ability to work a room at a cocktail party, but social

Adult	←	Who owns the problem?
↓		
Behaviour management use Adult and child responsible for outcome		
		S t o p
Consider solutions		T h i n k
Evaluate consequences 'What could we do?'		
Choose best solution 'Let's do it' Act!		D o
If it doesn't work, Stop and Think again or offer logical consequences		
'I feel… because (problem)'		**Stop**
'What could we try?'		**Think**
'Let's do it!'		**Do**

	Child

ocial skills training use Children responsible for utcome; adult facilitates

rge children not to react, just look and listen larify problem with child Reflect children's eelings 'You feel... because (problem)...'

onsider solutions with children

hildren evaluate consequences 'What could ou do?'

hildren choose best solution 'Do it' ncourage children to act!

ollow up. If it doesn't work, urge children to op and Think again

ou feel... because (problem)'

Vhat could you try?'

)o it!'

Draw three circles in a rectangle, like traffic lights, but don't colour them in. Get your child to colour in the red one, and as he does, explain the importance of stopping before leaping in and doing. When he has coloured it, write 'STOP before you act' next to it. Do the same with amber and green, writing 'THINK about what you will say and do' and 'DO be responsible for your actions' respectively. Put this somewhere your child will see it every day, and remind him to think of the traffic lights often.

skills refers to reading and interpreting social cues, having the ability to be in charge of your emotional reactions and behaving in an acceptable way. Not all children have difficulty with every aspect.

The steps opposite follow traffic-light symbols, and an

Here's an idea for you...

Defining idea...

Think like a man of action, act like a man of thought.

HENRI BERGSON, French philosopher

adult prompts children through each step:

- Red = Stop
- Amber = Think
- Green = Do

When confronted with a bully, kids should run through the mantra:

- Stop: identify your feelings.
- Think: you can choose to:

be cool

be co-operative

be naughty

be weak

- Do: what you decide.

This develops self-control, perceptual and communication skills primarily at Stop, cognitive problem solving skills at Think and behavioural skills at Do. Needy, clingy children are often stuck at Stop; they tend not to think or do much for themselves but continuously rely on others. Shy, anxious children are stuck at Think; they often think too much about what could happen and find it very difficult to choose what to do. Impulsive, aggressive children are stuck at Do; they do and do and rarely stop to think.

Q **My daughter gets very nervous about making decisions and can't make her mind up when it comes to the action stage. What can she do to make it easier?**

A *Kids who worry a lot tend to struggle with decision making too, as they think deeply about each consequence and become almost paralysed by ideas of what might happen. These children tend to be stuck at 'stop' or 'think'; they feel too intensely and because they think too much about what could happen, their ability to 'do' anything to cope is totally inhibited. You can address this by taking her through the 'stop' stage when she feels anxious and getting her to think through her problems with worries, and decide on an action that doesn't let the worries boss her around.*

Q **My son has Asperger's syndrome and is bullied because he is different. He doesn't seem to be able to do the 'think' stage. Any suggestions?**

A *Children with Asperger's do commonly struggle with thinking of options as they operate within a narrow, inflexible comfort zone. That said, I've used this with kids with Asperger's with good results. Lindy Petersen suggests that less emphasis is placed on brainstorming strategies at 'think' which leads kids with Asperger's off on unrelated or self-defensive tangents, or outside their comfort zone. She also advises putting more emphasis on the 'stop' and 'do' steps, linking the specific problem and choice of consequences.*

How did it go?

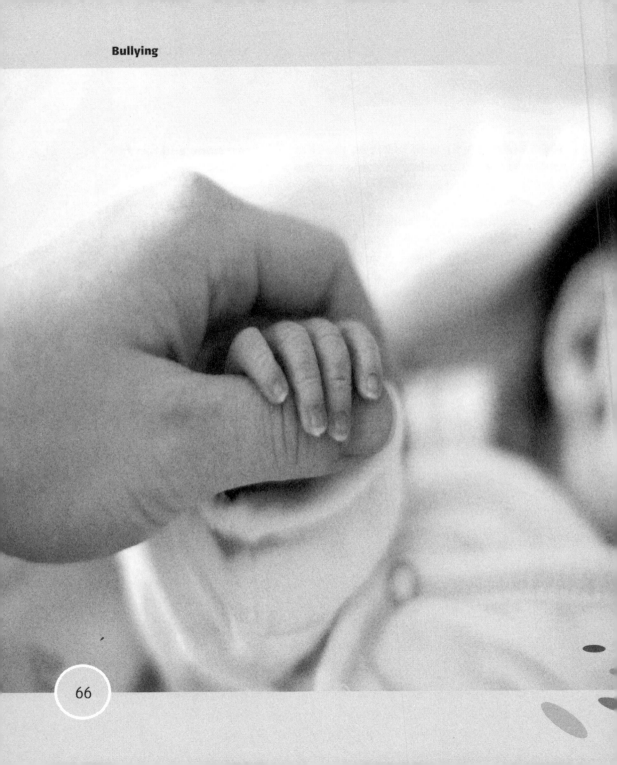

16

Roots of empathy

A visit from a baby has dramatically reduced bullying in schools in Canada, in Aboriginal communities in Australia, in New Zealand, the UK and the US.

When children are able to understand another person's point of view and respect their feelings, aggressive behaviour is less likely to occur. This has a direct impact on bullying.

Bringing a baby into class is a scientifically proven idea that reduces aggression and violence in classrooms. 'My class teacher is a baby' – no, it's not a slur on the teacher, but a comment on a quirky but amazingly effective programme which was developed in Canada by educator and parenting expert, Mary Gordon. In her 'roots of empathy' programme, a baby and one of his or her parents visit a school class every three weeks for an entire school year. The babies in the roots of empathy programme are between two and four months old at the start, as this age best enables the class to observe a wide range of an infant's development over the year, and there will be many changes to perceive and discuss.

A trained instructor helps the schoolchildren in the class observe their tiny teacher's development, celebrate any milestones, interact with their class baby and learn about an infant's needs and unique temperament. The instructor also visits before

Here's an idea for you...

Before children can fluently identify and describe their feelings, they need the right words to express them, so have a go at this. You can play this game with any number of players. Take it in turns to go through the alphabet, naming a feeling word which starts with each letter. The winner is the last person to name a word at their letter. For example, a is for afraid, b is for babyish, c is for cranky, d is for defeated, e is for excited...

and after each baby and parent visit to prepare the class and reinforce the learning from the last session. This powerful process helps children identify and reflect on their own feelings as well as the feelings of others. This is known as 'emotional literacy'. The term emotional literacy may sound a bit poncey, but it simply means the ability to describe and communicate feelings.

All the families who take part volunteer, and about a third of the parents who come into schools with their babies are fathers. The dads who take part in these sessions discuss their own feelings about being a parent as well as showing the class – through their actions towards the baby – exactly what it means to be a loving father. Boys in particular find this helpful when talking about their own feelings. It's especially the case for those boys who don't have strong male role models close to them or any other adult male confidants they can turn to.

Because babies aren't able to say how they are feeling, the children are invited to suggest the reasons why the baby might be upset, angry or happy and then to develop appropriate responses. As children learn to recognise the babies' feelings, they also learn how their own actions have an effect on other people. In short, they begin to develop empathy. Empathy requires children to see things from another person's perspective, so that the reasons behind another person's feeling, thinking and actions are understood.

A study in Venice looked at over 300 teenagers to see if there was a relationship between empathy and bullying. Low levels of empathy were found among those teenagers involved in bullying others. In contrast, higher levels of empathy were associated with the students who actively helped their victimised schoolmates. As levels of empathy rise, violence and aggression decrease. Many other studies have found that emotionally literate young people are less likely to physically, psychologically and emotionally hurt each other through bullying. So baby teachers can help on many levels.

Having a baby in the classroom is a positive twist on an age-old problem. When you begin to put yourself in someone else's shoes, you can start to work out those relationships with your peers as well.
JANEY TALBOT, community education co-ordinator, British Colombia

Defining idea...

The great gift of human beings is that we have the power of empathy.
MERYL STREEP

Defining idea...

How did it go?

Q **I'd love my kids to be involved in a formal programme like this but there isn't anything going on in the local area. Any suggestions?**

A *You have probably already asked your local education authorities about looking into setting up a programme like this – if not, then do so – but in the meantime, why not use this idea as a springboard? Think about ways in which you and your child could be together with a developing baby and have some conversations about what you both observe. Visiting a friend with a baby and talking together to the mum about how the baby may be feeling is a good start. Guessing at the baby's feelings will give your kids the words for discussing their own feelings, too.*

Q **I think it would be better to take the bullies aside for this sort of thing and let the other kids concentrate on schoolwork. Isn't this a waste of time for the children who don't have problems?**

A *This is all about increasing empathy in general, which in turn leads to lower levels of bullying and aggression. The people who have developed and evaluated it believe that it is actually successful because all children take part, instead of it merely targeting the bullies or aggressive children. Learning to identify and communicate feelings is an important part of everyone's schoolwork. Caring for living beings promotes problem-solving skills – and being aware of the onerous task of child raising may even prevent teenage pregnancies!*

17

I am what I am

Making a collage that expresses who you are helps you get to know yourself and feel better about yourself, too. It can also be great fun.

Bullying often seems to depersonalise people, making victims feel like robots, machinery or creatures from another planet. This is daunting, if not downright dehumanising.

Kids who have been bullied have lower self-esteem than kids who have not been bullied. The trick to feeling human again is rediscovering diversity. Bullies often target people precisely because of their differences. Because of this it can be difficult to enjoy your unique and special characteristics, the things that make you special, the things that make you – you.

An 'I am what I am' collage helps anyone celebrate who they are and feel proud of it. Think first about what you enjoy or value, what is special about you that you might want to share with others. Making this collage uses words and pictures to combine ideas about uniqueness that enable you to identify and delight in your individual talents, strengths and abilities.

Here's an idea for you...

Why not start taking some photos of yourself to include in your 'I am what I am' collage? As well as getting a nice pic of your face, ask someone to take photos of you when you are doing things that you enjoy.

Creating one of these collages is heaps of fun. You'll need a large piece of cardboard or other mounting board, scissors, glue, a stack of old magazines, comics, newspapers, coloured papers, stickers, sticky shapes, sequins, pom-poms, feathers, glitter, fabric scraps and any other general crafty bits you can get hold of. Go through the pile, clipping out words, pictures, perhaps photos of your favourite food, something in your favourite colour – anything that you feel shows what and who you are. You might want to focus on what you look like, what pets you have or what your family and friends are like, and what you enjoy doing. Think hard about what makes you unique. Lots of people find tearing things out of magazines has a wondrously soothing effect. As you tear things out, enjoy looking at the pictures and words that define you. These are your special strengths and attributes. Chances are you will also be tearing out things that reflect your values and interests.

Once you've worked your way through, and have a collection of papers and words, spread them out on a blank surface and work out how you'd like the collage to look. Don't be too neat; you can get some great effects by overlapping things you have cut or torn out, pasting pictures next to one another. Combining pictures to create something new is called montage. Try not to leave any space uncovered. Get the collage to look right before you stick any of the bits down on the board.

Next glue the pieces of paper and fabric onto the board to create your collage (remember to stick the bottom layer of pictures – if you're overlapping them – down first; it sounds obvious, but it's easy to get muddled). There are lots of different ways you can stick things down but the easiest is to use a stick-based glue, as this is fast, not too messy and as easy to use as a pen. If you have a lot of heavy paper or photographs, you might like to use a mount spray which you can buy in art and craft shops. Mount sprays can be messier, but give you even glue coverage.

Don't let anyone tell you, you have to be a certain way. Be unique. Be what you feel.
MELISSA ETHERIDGE, American singer

Defining idea...

My top tips? If you can't find images to match your ideas about yourself, draw a picture. I suggest you also find a photograph of yourself that you really like, where you look relaxed and happy. Cut it out and place yourself in the middle of your collage. Some people like to include a motto or an inspirational phrase to keep their spirits up during tough times. If you find a quote that you would like to live by, why not add it to your collage?

Once you have made your collage, hang it somewhere you'll see it often. When you're feeling down, look at it to be reminded of what makes you special and individual, and what you can feel proud of. Whatever the bullies do, they can't take that feeling away.

Know that although in the eternal scheme of things you are small, you are also unique and irreplaceable.
MARGARET LAURENCE, writer

Defining idea...

How did it go?

Q **I'm not very good at craft stuff and any type of making. It isn't one of my special unique skills. I prefer computers. I'm looking for a way to still get the benefits of this idea. Can you suggest something?**

A *Actually, it sounds as though your computer skills would be perfectly suited to doing this. Instead of getting a stack of magazines and lots of glue, cut and paste pictures from websites and use lots of different fonts to create a collage which you could print or use as a screensaver.*

Q **I'm an eight-year-old schoolboy and I was bullied badly in my last school. I'm moving to a new school and I've been thinking about sharing this collage with my new class so they will know a bit about me before I start. My dad thinks this might make me stick out again and that people might know too much about me and could pick on me. Any suggestions?**

A *Perhaps you and your dad sharing this idea with your new teacher first is your best option. Often teachers will make this an activity for the whole class so the members of the class can get to know themselves and each other better. This way you can still share your collage but won't stand out, as everyone will be doing the same thing.*

18

Mobile phone harassment

It's a Gr8 way 2 tlk 2 friends, but it can also be a Gr8 way 4 bullies 2 hurt U.

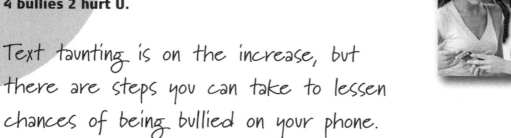

Text taunting is on the increase, but there are steps you can take to lessen chances of being bullied on your phone.

Malicious calls are a serious crime and nobody need suffer in silence. There's a lot you can do to stop them happening.

Mobile phone use by young people has increased exponentially in recent years. In Germany, 92% of twelve to nineteen year olds and 47% of six to thirteen year olds own a mobile phone. For the most part, this is a great thing, as kids can stay in touch with friends and family and also let someone know if they are in trouble. Unfortunately, mobile phones carry risks too. According to a UK survey, 14% of children have been bullied on their mobile.

Bullying by phone can take several forms including receiving a phone call or text message that says things that are insulting or threatening, receiving one that's distressing or intimidating or having your phone used by someone else for a nasty purpose. It can also mean receiving a photo or video message that is rude or offensive, getting a text message made of letters and numbers formed into offensive pictures or being bombarded by a large volume of text messages or calls.

Here's an idea for you...

Limit your mobile phone use. It might sound old-fashioned, but think about using landlines only for a while. It can feel as if this is giving in to the bully, but the less you use your phone, the more frustrated your text bully will become, and she's likely to give up.

Unfortunately, with pay as you go phones, it's easy for bullies to send texts and make calls while appearing anonymous. Despite this, there are things you can do to reduce and eliminate phone bullying.

First of all, rest those tempted thumbs and don't reply to texts from people you don't know. In some cases, bullies send out random texts and wait to see who responds. Another reason for not replying is that if you complain about the bullying, replying can delay any investigations.

As soon as any phone bullying starts, get help immediately from an adult you trust. Bullies operate outside social norms and will try to isolate and separate you from friends, family and parents, but don't be fooled. If you're tempted to flick back a message like 'Y R U doing this to me?', you'd be giving the bullies exactly what they want. Bullies get their kicks from provoking a response from you, so no response deprives them of their goal. Instead of replying, save the text. Saving bullying texts means you can build up evidence – so if you need to involve the police, you can give them the proof they need. It's also a good idea to keep any itemised phone bills.

If you receive abusive or upsetting calls, stay calm and try not to show emotion. Hang up. If you get a call from an unrecognised number, don't say anything when you answer the phone. A genuine caller will speak first. A malicious caller will probably hang up. These calls are a criminal offence in most countries. Almost all malicious calls can now be traced whether they come from private, public or even mobile phones.

If the bullying continues, consider getting a second mobile phone. This can be an expensive option, but if you're really stumped, it could be the smart thing to do. Be really picky about who you give the new number to, and keep a written record of who has it. When you give friends your new number, make sure they understand it is for their exclusive use, and that they can't pass it on to other people. If the bullying keeps going even on your second phone, you will have a list of likely culprits. Finally, don't flash your phone about. If there's a lock facility on it, choose a secret number so that the keypad is locked when you're not using it. If someone you don't know asks to borrow your phone to make a quick call tell them that it's out of credit and only accepts incoming calls.

> *I don't own a cell phone or a pager. I just hang around everyone I know, all the time. If someone wants to get a hold of me, they just say 'Mitch,' and I say 'what?' and turn my head slightly.*
> MITCH HEDBERG, American comedian

Defining idea...

How did it go?

Q **I've been bombarded with texts that are mildly threatening but not grossly offensive. It's the volume rather than the content that bothers me. Is there anything that my mobile phone company could do?**

A *Yes. They can send a warning to the bully. In some cases they will provide a change of number. If things get serious and you involve the police, the mobile phone company can also help with law enforcement. Every time a mobile phone is switched on or off it sends a signal to the nearest mast and, although the caller may have concealed their number from you, this is information which phone companies will have on their system. It's then easy for the police to find out the culprit's phone number.*

Q **My friend has been accused of bullying by text after sending a funny photo of another friend in fancy dress. He is very upset as he feels he was joking around, and it was misinterpreted. What can he do?**

A *A joke can easily go from funny to offensive, and when people are angry or excited we can say or do things by text that we regret later. Everyone needs to be careful when sending texts. Your friend may not have intended to cause hurt but it sounds as if he has inadvertently done so. An apology to the person who feels hurt is always a good first step. These two rules should keep him – and everyone else – out of further trouble: before pressing 'send' ask yourself if someone could be hurt or offended by the message, and never, ever send a photo or video of another person without their permission.*

19

In class

Does your child's school have anti-bullying guidelines or rules about bullying? Is it just lip service or does it really work? Discover which strategies make a difference.

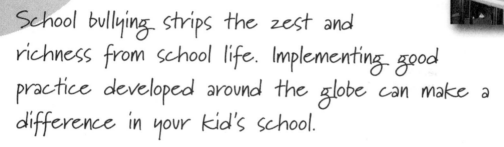

School bullying strips the zest and richness from school life. Implementing good practice developed around the globe can make a difference in your kid's school.

Many schools have an anti-bullying policy and in some countries, like the UK, this is mandatory. However, it is often difficult to know which strategies actually help and which might make things worse. There are a few things to look out for if your school has an anti-bullying policy. If it doesn't, you can learn from some leading international ruses to help set one up that is truly effective.

You can tell if an anti-bullying programme is likely to be effective if it has been tested on many children and studied by researchers. Good anti-bullying programmes are based on a sound theoretical framework or a guiding philosophy, providing theoretical evidence about how the programme is supposed to reduce bullying.

Lessons from Norway
Norway pioneered a successful bullying intervention in Bergen the 1980s, following the suicides of three boys. Supported by Norway's National Ministry of Education,

Here's an idea for you...

Even if the school already has an anti-bullying policy, it's a good idea to start a group to co-ordinate this, so that it doesn't just gather dust in a drawer. School-based bullying prevention works best when co-ordinated by a team including an administrator, a teacher from each year, a member of the support staff, a school nurse, counsellor or mental health professional and a parent. The team should meet regularly to review findings from the school's survey, plan specific bullying prevention activities, motivate staff, students and parents, and ensure that the efforts continue over time.

this programme puts particular emphasis on peer aggression and ill-treatment. It was rolled out throughout schools in Norway after being shown to reduce levels of bullying. Between 1983 to 1985, the programme was evaluated among 2500 students (between eleven and fourteen years of age) from forty-two schools. Eight months after the intervention, researchers found that there was a significant reduction (up to 50%) in bullying.

The Bergen programme had done several things. It increased teacher, parent and student awareness of the problems of peer aggression and victimisation, and tried to encourage active involvement of adults and peers in resolving bully/victim incidents. It also gave widespread consideration to serious talks with bullies, victims and the parents of bullied children. Links with social workers and school psychologists were encouraged for expert advice with more severe bullying.

Lessons from England

In the early 1990s, the Sheffield Anti-Bullying Project was set up in over twenty schools, reaching out to 6500 students aged between eight and sixteen. It was based on the principles of the Bergen intervention, but schools also had the choice to implement playground interventions or to work directly one to one with bullies and victims.

Victimisation rates decreased by 14% in primary schools and by 7% in secondary schools. Bullying rates decreased by 12% in primary schools and by 12% in secondary schools. The proportion of pupils who told a teacher about bullying increased by 6% in primary schools and by 32% in secondary schools; the proportion of bullies reporting that a teacher had talked to them about it increased by 5% in primary schools and by 38% in secondary schools.

> *In the first place God made idiots; that was for practice; then he made school boards.*
> MARK TWAIN

Defining idea...

Lessons from Spain

The Sevilla Anti-Violencia Escolar (SAVE) project took place in Seville between 1995 and 1996 and again from 1999 to 2000. SAVE was based on the work carried out in Sheffield and Bergen but was developed independently. Ten schools took part in SAVE, which had four parts:

- The democratic management of interpersonal relationships.
- Co-operative group work and the curriculum.
- Training in emotions, attitudes and values.
- Direct interventions for pupils at risk of or involved in bullying.

Here the number of victimised pupils decreased by 57%, and the number of bullying pupils decreased by 16%.

Lessons for your school

Have a look at your school's anti-bullying strategy. Does it follow principles that have been shown to work internationally? Is there anything else that could be incorporated? If your school doesn't have one, or if there's room for improvement, why not brainstorm what an ideal strategy might look like and present this to the headteacher?

How did it go?

Q **After the tragic suicide of a bullied teenager, our son's school has stepped up their anti-bullying efforts. They've been following the Bergen principles, and are getting good at incorporating anti-bullying messages into the curriculum. I'm the parent representative for my son's year and have been asked if there is anything else that the parent group would like to see happening. What can you recommend?**

A *It really does sound as if they are making admirable efforts in light of this heartbreaking event. Why not encourage teachers to give over some class time to bullying prevention? Kids benefit especially from a regular period of time to talk about bullying. As well as empowering children, these sessions mean teachers can stay attuned to any covert bullying and unvoiced classroom concerns.*

Q **I'm a mother and a teacher, and have been interested to read some of this research about bullying. In the examples cited, interventions seemed to be time limited over months or years. What is the optimum amount of time an anti-bullying intervention should run for in order for it to be effective in a school?**

A *That's a great question. For research purposes, interventions are frequently time based so that scientists can look at what was happening in school before an intervention and compare that to bullying and victimisation levels afterwards. In the real world, there isn't a 'use by' date for bullying prevention. These anti-bullying initiatives ought to be perpetual and become a seamless, indefinite part of the curriculum.*

20

A friend in need

Bullies are more likely to pick on kids who don't have many friends. But what if you don't have anyone special to share your thoughts, dreams and fun time?

They say the best way to make a friend is to be one. Find out how.

Friends are great. They help immunise you against the effects of bullying. Some children naturally attract friends, but many others have to work a little harder at it. Kids who are sensitive or shy are often in the latter group, and these are, unfortunately, also the types of children who are more likely to be bullied. The trouble is that you can easily lose your confidence when it comes to making friends if you've been bullied. But that confidence can soon come back. Here are a few suggestions that might help, but don't rush into them all at once. A friendship can take time to develop; start at the beginning and take it from there.

Firstly, try to define what makes a good friend. It might be someone who is smiley and approachable. Or someone kind and helpful, who isn't judgemental. Maybe it's someone who is fair or good at organising games and things to do. Think about someone you know who has these qualities. What do they like to do? You could try some of the same things. If they skate, go to the skate park; if they go to a swimming club, you could join. Just be friendly, and say hello. And don't only think about that particular person, either – there will be other interesting people you could get to know as well.

Here's an idea for you...

Good listeners make good friends. Your mouth can get you into trouble with friends, but your ears never will. If a friend confides in you about bullying, hear them out, without interrupting, giving your opinion or telling them about your experiences. Check from time to time that you have understood what they are saying. Rather than offering advice, give them a chance to work things out for themselves as they talk.

After a bit, someone in the group will probably ask you if you want to do something with them. Now, while you're getting to know everyone, it's a good idea to go along with what they want to do, even if it isn't exactly the sort of thing you'd prefer. For instance, if they all want to see a movie, and you'd rather see a different one, go to their choice on the first occasion.

People are often worried about what to say to new friends, but the real trick is being a good listener. Many people are better at talking, so a group of potential friends will really value someone who listens carefully to them. When you're working out who to confide in, and who you can trust, it pays to experiment by telling people some stuff that isn't that important, like what pets you have and what jobs your parents have. If they don't gossip with simple information, they're likely to be more trustworthy with serious and private stuff too. If you're asked to give your opinion, be honest. If you pretend to be someone else, it gets exhausting and your new friends don't get a chance to get to know the real you.

When you do start to confide in your new friends, ask them stuff about themselves too. That makes conversations feel very equal and reduces the chances that they might feel you are dumping your worries on them. If you have talked about something serious or upsetting, try to make a big effort to talk about something cheerier next time. It can feel like a real mission to find positive things to talk about, but it is important for friendships that you make the effort, as even best friends don't want to be burdened by talking about your problems and worries all the time. It can make them feel as if you need them to solve problems and people can be put off. I don't at all mean that you can't talk to friends about bullying, just that you need to remember to talk about other things too.

The antidote for fifty enemies is one friend.
ARISTOTLE

Defining idea...

Some people go to priests; others to poetry; I to my friends.
VIRGINIA WOOLF

Defining idea...

85

How did it go?

Q **A girl I think could become a friend hangs out with her mates in the mall at weekends. I tried hanging around there too, but they made sarcastic comments about me and I felt crappy. What did I do wrong?**

A *Probably nothing. Some people aren't worth being friends with. If these girls were mean to you when you approached them, then they're probably not going to be good friends anyway. It is really disheartening when something like this happens, but please don't let it put you off. It can be intimidating approaching a big group, so have you thought about a smaller group of friends you might like to be part of? Some people find it easier to make friends when doing an activity like art or swimming or cycling, so that might also be an idea you could follow up.*

Q **I was bullied in my previous school. We moved house and I've had a fresh start but I'm struggling to make friends in my new school. A lot of the kids wear a particular brand of shoes and only seem to like kids who look the part. My mum says she doesn't want to be pressured into buying special trainers just so I can be accepted. Any suggestions?**

A *It sounds as if you've had a really rough time. Your mum has your best interests at heart – it may seem terribly shallow and you shouldn't need shoes to be accepted – but you do need to feel you can fit in. Appearances are important and it would be great if she could allow you to have the same shoes as almost everybody else is wearing, if at all possible. It may give you a chance to become part of the group, after all.*

21

Help you can call on

If you want to speak to someone about being bullied, but can't face speaking to a parent or teacher, consider calling a helpline.

Trained counsellors are available at the end of the phone to help with bullying-related problems. You don't have to give your name, or say any more than you want to.

I went to school with Alexa Varah. When we were about ten or eleven years old, she took part in a memorable school assembly and talked about her grandfather, the Anglican vicar Chad Varah. Some people may recognise his name as that of the founder of the Samaritans, the first confidential telephone listening service. Reverend Varah had been inspired to set up the Samaritans after officiating at the funeral of a fourteen-year-old girl. He felt strongly that things would have been very different if she had been able to confide in someone. He was an amazing man; because of the work he started, telephone helplines have evolved and grown.

My husband's godmother is a famous Swedish children's writer and television producer, Gunnel Linde. Among her many achievements was setting up the world's first telephone helpline intended specifically for kids. Her idea was so successful that it has been adopted around the world and many countries now have a free confidential telephone helpline for children and young people worried about bullying.

Here's an idea for you...

Why not find out what telephone helplines are available for any young people being bullied in your area? Store the number somewhere safe and accessible but private, perhaps in your mobile phone if you have one, and then it is always there for you to access should you suddenly need someone to speak to.

Both Chad Varah and Gunnel Linde realised that sometimes people need alternatives to the conventional sources of help. If you don't feel brave enough to speak to somebody face to face, then an anonymous telephone helpline can be a valuable first step. Make no mistake, it can be really difficult to confide in someone else about bullying. Many kids worry about burdening their parents or are concerned that they might not be believed; other kids worry that telling a parent or teacher might make the bullying that they are currently enduring even worse. So they keep all this stuff to themselves.

Calling a telephone helpline about bullying is a vital opportunity to express your feelings. For many young people it is the first time they have spoken about what they are experiencing, and just telling someone else and being taken seriously is a huge relief. Speaking to a stranger on the phone about bullying is an opportunity to think about your options, as well. Two heads are almost always better than one, and drawing on the expertise and experience of someone who has helped other bullied kids can help you make an informed decision about whether or not to tell any adults you know. Speaking first on the phone means you have a sense of control over the pace of any bullying information you share, should you decide to confide in a teacher or parent. Remember that you only have to give as much information as feels comfortable when you call, too. If you are asked your name, and don't want to give it, you can choose a different one or just give your first name. It doesn't matter; it's down to you.

Now, there are some disadvantages of calling a helpline which you should be prepared for, but they shouldn't stop you calling. Sometimes lines get busy, and although in theory you can speak to someone when it suits you, everyone else with a bullying problem might be trying to ring at just that time. If you do have trouble getting through, persevere and, if you can, call back at a different time of day when things may be quieter. Another potential drawback is that you might speak to someone in detail, only to call back on another occasion and have to start from scratch with someone else. This is less likely to happen when you confide in somebody face to face. If this is something you're worried about, ask the helpline if they keep notes or if it would be possible to speak to the same person next time. Different places do things differently, but it does make sense to ask because it can feel quite overwhelming to have to start a long and painful story over and over again.

The telephone is a good way to talk to people without having to offer them a drink.
FRAN LEBOWITZ, American writer and humorist

Defining idea...

91

How did it go?

Q **I'm worried that if I call a bullying helpline, the number will show up on our phone bill and my parents will find out. Is there any way I can stop this happening?**

A *Some helplines, like Childline in the UK, are free, and the number doesn't show up on the phone bill. Other helplines might show up on your bill, so it is worth finding out beforehand – by making the first call from a public phone box and asking them directly. You could also use a pay as you go mobile phone, of course, rather than a land line.*

Q **I have the number of the Samaritans, but I'm not feeling suicidal. Can I still call them about my problems?**

A *Although the Samaritans were originally set up to help people in crisis who felt like ending their lives, they do take calls from people who are not so far down the line and they don't hang up on anyone at all. However, my suggestion would be that you find a dedicated line for children and young people, where counsellors will be specially trained and have particular skills which can help you.*

22

No blame

This no-blame approach comes from New Zealand's national anti-bullying programme, Kia Kaha.

Kia Kaha is a Maori term and means 'stand strong', and that's just what it aims to encourage.

This programme was set up in New Zealand as a joint venture between the police and New Zealand Telecom. Although it is predominantly a school-based programme, its 'no-blame' idea can be adapted for many other settings. It acknowledges that the vast majority of kids are not involved in bullying. They neither bully nor are victims. However, even though these kids know bullying is wrong, they frequently silently collude with the ill-treatment they also know is going on.

The no-blame approach involves these bystanders in stopping bullying behaviour. It starts with the understanding that it is more important to solve the problem of bullying than to punish perpetrators. It draws on principles developed by George Robinson and Barbara Maines, and has four key features – the absence of blame, an encouragement of empathy, shared responsibility and problem solving.

In Sweden, psychologist Dr Anatol Pikas developed a similar approach, called Shared Concern. He advocated a series of brief conversations with children involved in bullying. He suggested that the children doing the bullying should be spoken to first, before those who had been bullied. He also recommended that these talks should not be confrontational.

Here's an idea for you...

Why not use a school staff meeting to present this no-blame approach and suggest trying it out for a term? If you are a parent or young person, why not ask if you can attend a staff meeting at your school to present this idea?

In New Zealand, the no-blame process is usually run by a professional like a school guidance counsellor. Here are the stages and the steps they take.

1. Interview the person being bullied

- Support them and congratulate them on speaking out.
- Assure them that the bullying is not their fault and that they do not deserve to be bullied.
- Discuss how it feels to be bullied.
- Invite them to write down their feelings about being bullied.
- Explore any possible behaviours of their own where they may act more decisively to increase their own confidence in the situation.
- Tell them you are going to work with other people involved and some others in the group/class to get them to understand the effect that bullying or a lack of support is having on one of their classmates.
- Ask them for the names of people they would like included in the group.

2. Assemble a group of people

- Ask the advice of teachers who know the class or peer group well and can remain objective.
- Include the person who has been doing the bullying and his or her two main supporters.
- Include one or two bystanders who have been friends of the victim in the past.
- Include two dominant, assertive group/class members who have observed the bullying but done nothing to stop it in the past.

3. Convene a meeting of the group

- Do not include the victim.
- Allow at least thirty minutes.
- Seat everyone in a circle.
- Explain the problem and share the feelings the victim has written down.
- Discuss why the victim is feeling this way.
- Don't apportion blame. This will allow the group to respond objectively to the bullying and to help find a solution.
- Talk about group responsibility for helping solve this problem.
- Encourage each group member to suggest positive ways the victim could be made happier.
- Say you will leave it up to the group to do these things to support the victim.
- Set a time for reconvening in a week (or other appropriate period of time) to review progress.

4. Continue to support the victim

- Meet with the victim informally once a day.
- Ensure the ongoing safety of the victim.

5. Reconvene the group in a week

- Discuss progress on doing the things they agreed to do.
- Praise them for any changes you have noticed.

All blame is a waste of time. No matter how much fault you find with another, and regardless of how much you blame him, it will not change you. The only thing blame does is to keep the focus off you when you are looking for external reasons to explain your unhappiness or frustration. You may succeed in making another feel guilty about something by blaming him, but you won't succeed in changing whatever it is about you that is making you unhappy.
WAYNE DYER, footballer

Defining idea...

95

How did it go?

Q   **I have heard that there is some controversy about this approach, in particular that it reinforces the idea that bullying is OK and has no bad consequences. What's your view?**

A   *You're right, the idea hasn't been universally adopted and some anti-bullying campaigners have been vociferous in their opposition to the no-blame approach. Their chief complaint is that it does not encourage bullies to own and confront their actions. These people feel that blaming approaches are more likely to induce remorse and encourage the bullies to take responsibility for their actions. Rather than belong to the 'hanging's too good for them' crew, I take a more pragmatic approach. It might not reform every bully, but if it helps victims, I'm for it. I've seen bullies moved when they've realised how much they've hurt or upset someone, and even take spontaneous steps to try to make amends for their actions.*

Q   **I really don't like the sound of bullies getting away with it. Shouldn't they be made to face up to what they have done wrong?**

A   *It seems that you've misunderstood the ethos of the idea, which many people do. Although the no-blame approach isn't a fact-finding or fault-finding mission, it does encourage reflection on what has happened. If nothing was done, it might be construed as bullies 'being let off'. Instead this approach helps both bullies and victims.*

23

Fake it till you make it

Acting as if bullying doesn't matter is an important step towards getting rid of bullies. If they believe you don't care, they'll move elsewhere.

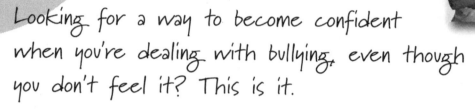

Looking for a way to become confident when you're dealing with bullying, even though you don't feel it? This is it.

Bullies tend to pick on kids who aren't very confident, and then they strip them of what little confidence they had in the first place. The upshot of this is that a lot of kids feel they won't be able to stand up to bullies or change their responses to them until they become more confident. It sounds logical but, actually, this line of thinking is topsy-turvy.

Even when you're not feeling at all confident when facing a bully, you need to look and sound as if you are. We become confident when we know what to do and are as sure as we can be that it's going to go well.

Think about something you are really good at. It might be riding a bike, or playing the ukulele. Cast your mind back to when you first started. The chances are that you felt a little nervous and maybe even a bit clueless to begin with. Then you picked up a few basic skills. But to progress to the level that you've now achieved,

Here's an idea for you...

When I run groups for bullied children, we practise 'fake it till you make it' as a role play. You can do this at home too. You need at least two people, but the more the merrier. One person needs to pretend to be a bully, the other pretends to be a confident person who sees the bully off. Brothers and sisters can be bystanders who observe how good the bullied person is at faking it. Encourage them to give feedback and make suggestions.

you will have gone beyond your comfort zone, many times, pushing yourself and reaching higher goals. What was uppermost in your mind? Persistence, perhaps, or practise or perseverance. It's likely to have been one of these, rather than confidence – that tends to come after a skill has been mastered.

The good news is that bravado is easier to muster than confidence. Bill Gates, the founder of Microsoft, faked it till he made it. When he was a student at Harvard, news broke about the world's first potentially commercial computer, the Altair. The computer was good, and it worked, but it lacked its own programming language. Bill Gates called the Altair's maker and told him that he and a fellow student had written a programming language that would work on it. They hadn't. He promised that they would bring it in the next holiday. For the next two months, the pair worked tirelessly, and probably didn't feel all that confident as they didn't even have an Altair to practise on. The moment of truth arrived when they tested the software on the Altair for the first time – when demonstrating it to the man who'd created the machine. I imagine they felt very nervous, but they had to look confident and act as if they knew what they were doing. It worked and the rest, as they say, is history.

The trick that Bill Gates used, and that you can use too, is to pretend that you already have skills, and act as if you do. So when you are not feeling confident, just fake it that you already have the confidence to act as if bullying doesn't bother you, or to front up to bullies in other ways. Faking it repeatedly will help it stick. And, harsh as it sounds, you're unlikely to become a confident person who stands up to bullies until you pretend to be that person first.

Believe you can and you're halfway there.
THEODORE ROOSEVELT

Defining idea...

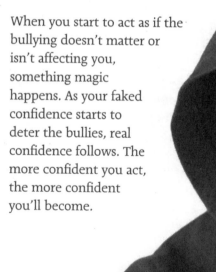

When you start to act as if the bullying doesn't matter or isn't affecting you, something magic happens. As your faked confidence starts to deter the bullies, real confidence follows. The more confident you act, the more confident you'll become.

How did it go?

Q **I have been so upset by bullying that I can't bring myself to take part in any 'fake it till you make it' role play with my mum. We've tried, but it's as if I just forget it's her pretending to bully me, and I get very tearful. Is there another way I can practise?**

A *It's not uncommon for children to be so damaged by bullying that they want to avoid anything that reminds them of it. Unfortunately, avoiding what we fear makes things worse in the long run. I suggest that you flip roles, with you playing the bully and your mum playing a victim who will demonstrate some positive, confident reactions. Many kids who have previously not been able to take part in role play are able to do so once roles are reversed and find that playing the bully gives them a sense of power and fun. You'll probably also gain new insight into how bullies behave, and a chance to see confidence in the face of bullying, all of which will help you fake it till you make it.*

Q **I've tried acting confident, but it feels really weird and not at all like me. I don't see why the bullies should make me act like someone else. I want to be myself, and acting like a confident person makes me feel funny. What can I do?**

A *Well done for taking the first step and going outside your comfort zone. Lots of people find it feels strange and different at first. And you probably will feel like a dork when you first try this. But remember, if you persevere, you won't have to fake it for long, and you will become confident and accomplished. A few uncomfortable feelings at the start are probably worth it.*

24

Take a hike

Many bullying experts tell kids to just walk away. Kids tell me it's not that easy. Here's how to walk away and look confident.

It's hard for someone to bully you if you're not there. But walking away from a bully can be one of the hardest things to do.

Bullies get their thrills from watching kids fight back, get upset or annoyed. They love nothing more than a big reaction. Walking away shows a bully that you're not interested in a fight or in any confrontation whatsoever, physical or verbal. When you've just been shouted at or picked on, you're not likely to be feeling very brave or confident, but walking as if you are feeling like the ballsiest kid in school means bullies are much less likely to pick on you. Walking with confidence means keeping your eyes up, your body straight and using strong, purposeful movements. Head high and shoulders back is the look you are aiming for – like a strutting catwalk model.

You can either say something, like 'stop bullying me' or 'please stop doing that', and then walk away, or you can just walk away without saying anything at all. The trick to walking away powerfully is to walk away as if you don't care, even when you care a lot. Looking nonchalant as you walk off unsettles bullies as it isn't what they expect to happen. You might be tempted to sneak away quietly, but walking a little

Practice makes perfect. This quick drill will help you walk away with confidence. You already know that bullies look for easy targets, why not make it a bit harder for them and look like a tough target instead? Do this by standing as straight as you can, holding your head high, relaxing your shoulders back and making eye contact. Then turn around smoothly and walk away, looking poised. If you practise this drill until it feels like second nature, you'll be able to walk away calmly if you are bullied.

faster than feels comfortable makes you seem more confident than you feel because it looks as if you are striding along with a purpose. And nothing says 'I'm not confident' like slouching, so stand straight. Smiling also makes you look self-assured, by the way. As you walk away from the bullies, make eye contact with the first non-bully you come across and give that person a broad smile. It may be the last thing you feel like doing, but it helps.

It can be difficult; walking away feels unnatural at first because your natural tendencies when confronted with danger are to either run away or fight back. Before walking away, take a deep breath in, and as you take your first few steps away, breathe out slowly. This will help you feel calm. While you are walking, say something positive to yourself in your head like, 'I'm a cool person' or 'I am better than these bullies'. These sorts of upbeat phrases help you feel better inside and that will come across in your body language as you walk.

Once you have turned your back on a bully, walk calmly to a safe place. Turning your back might feel like the last thing you should be doing, but it can be effective. If you're in school, go to a classroom or to the staff room. If you're outside, go somewhere where you can find an adult. You don't have to tell anyone what has happened, but if the bullies see you approaching adults, they are more likely to leave you alone.

If you see someone else being bullied, you also need to walk away – and get help. Again, you can tell the bully to stop it at first, but if you don't feel like doing that, it's OK to just walk away and get an adult. If you stand and watch someone else being bullied without walking away, it makes the bullies feel even more powerful as they have an audience to show off to. You might not mean to encourage a bully, but many people accidentally do just that – they encourage more bullying by being bystanders and not walking away.

No problem is so formidable that you can't walk away from it.
CHARLES SCHULZ, the creator of *Peanuts*

Defining idea...

How did
it go?

Q **I've tried walking away but the bullies just stood in my way and pushed me. They were all laughing at me and I couldn't get away. What could I have done?**

A *If this happens again, try telling the bullies politely that you want to pass; they might just be surprised and let you. Above all, it's important to avoid the dance of dodging back and forth, getting more and more upset. Instead, use an element of surprise. Stand still, look bored and then make a sudden dash for it. When you can't walk away, run. Again, run to a place where you'll find adults. Another ruse is to agree with the mean things bullies are saying, then walk away. They are often so startled that you have agreed with their insults that it gives you a chance to walk away. It doesn't mean all that stuff is true; it's just a trick to get you out of there.*

Q **When I start to walk away something funny happens and I just start running and I can't stop until I am somewhere safe like home or in the classroom. I wish I could act cool and walk away calmly. I don't want the bully to think I am running away. Can you help?**

A *Actually, it sounds like an excellent response. Don't worry about your speed. The main thing is that you are getting away. It's much harder for bullies to pick on you if you don't stand still, so keep moving.*

25

Peace games

War games like battleships are almost as universal as bullying. They teach kids strategy, tactics and a desire to win. But what games teach them about respect, justice and peace?

Discover some peace games that will help kids learn to resolve conflicts and communicate more effectively to make better friends.

Children learn through play. A playful attitude and outlook doesn't hurt adults either. Playing these five peace games is a great way of changing opinions and discovering conflict resolution skills, both of which are useful ways of coping with bullies. The first thing about games is that they should be fun, so whatever you plan to play, put on some music, roll back the rug and don't worry about looking silly.

Silent jigsaws

Work in pairs or larger groups to complete a jigsaw, but without speaking. Try this first with a fairly simple one, as the four-million-piece, black-on-black puzzles will just have everyone tearing their hair out, which isn't fun or peaceful. Doing a simple jigsaw together in silence helps build co-operative non-verbal communication skills, even when you're teamed with stiff and slightly tricky people. You'll find they improve as they just have to get on with it.

Here's an idea for you...

There are now a number of online games where the goal is countering bloodshed instead of creating it. The themes are diverse, ranging from combating genocide and ending world hunger to bringing about peace in the Middle East. Games like this instil positive ideals about social justice, help bring about creative responses to conflict, improve social skills and aren't bad for hand–eye co-ordination either. New ones are being developed all the time, so get Googling and gaming.

Good news

A group of kids spends a week reading the newspapers (yes, really) and cuts out examples of war and conflict. They then bring these back to the group and discuss peaceful ways of resolving the conflict together. If you can come up with diverse suggestions, and also apply them to common bullying scenarios too, so much the better. This activity helps build – you've guessed it – conflict resolution skills.

Loo roll game

This is a lovely, daft game to help develop peaceful, co-operative team building among classmates or other groups. You will need at least ten players, six years old and upwards, and two rolls of loo paper. Get everyone to sit in a circle, and open the circle out until everyone can make eye contact with everyone else in the circle. Choose someone in the circle to be the start point, by holding the end of the loo roll while the roll is unrolled going over the heads of everyone in the circle clockwise without breaking. When the roll reaches the starting point, it's time to pass it back, this time through everyone's legs. If either when passing over heads or through legs, the roll breaks, the roll has to be returned to the starting point and the team has to start again. You can either race the clock or another circular team. This game can feel a bit ridiculous, but it helps build patience, fast yet skilful communication, endurance and diplomatic negotiation skills.

It's on the cards

Get the children to write down all the different ways someone their age could be bullied or has been bullied. Now ask them to put each idea on an index card. When they've done this, encourage them to decorate the cards with stickers or glitter pens (you can skip this stage but these cards are so much jazzier if you embellish them and doing so makes the game feel more creative and fun). Then get the group to think about all the different ways they could respond to the suggestion on each card. I suggest you have a small prize, like a lolly, for the best or most original answer for each round. No prizes for identifying what this game teaches you.

Peace is not something you wish for, it's something you make. Something you do, something you are, something you give away.
ROBERT FULGHUM, author of *All I Really Need to Know I Learned in Kindergarten*

Defining idea...

Peace is not an absence of war, it is a virtue, a state of mind, a disposition for benevolence, confidence, justice.
BARUCH SPINOZA

Defining idea...

Blind walking

My husband Peter introduced me to blind walking, a game he has played with many groups to build trust. You play it in pairs. One person has to close their eyes or is blindfolded. This person is the blind walker. The other person keeps their eyes open and leads the blind walker around a room or garden, around obstacles and around other pairs of blind walkers. After a while, swap roles. This builds not only trust but co-operation as well.

How did
it go?

Q **My daughter and her friend did the silent jigsaw puzzle – but finished up having the mother of all arguments and were really mean to each other. My daughter says that not being able to talk was awful, and that her friend was doing it all wrong and she just couldn't bear it. Where did we go wrong?**

A *Oh, no! It's vital to have some patience when doing silent jigsaws. It won't be as fast as usual but if you keep in mind that the goal is communication, rather than completion, they ought to be able to relax and have fun with it.*

Q **We like the idea of the loo roll game but are trying to be green in our school and this seems rather wasteful. Any suggestions?**

A *I agree; it isn't the greenest of games, but perhaps you might be persuaded to try it with recycled loo roll? And it could always be collected up, even in pieces, and returned to the loos afterwards.*

26

Shielding yourself

When it feels as if they're on the front line, battling bullies endlessly, having a shield to fend off the attacks can make a huge difference to younger kids.

This simple visualisation technique is great; helping kids create imaginary defences can effectively combat teasing.

Remember the old adage, sticks and stones may break my bones but names will never hurt me? It's baloney. Teasing and taunting can be impossible to ignore. Verbal bullying can be especially painful because it feels like constant criticism and it can be difficult to argue back against it.

A bully shield can help children who are not quick with verbal retorts cope with taunts and also look more confident to bullies. Kids who have been bullied can imagine that they have a special shield which is both bullet proof and bully proof, and which sends nasty remarks back to the person who said them. Visualisation is an especially powerful tool for younger kids. They usually have better visual skills than verbal ones, and the process of slowing down to imagine and visualise helps calm them down too.

Prepare your child by running through this routine with them: next time you are likely to come across a bully, close your eyes and imagine that you are strapping your shield on in preparation. Think about how high the shield is and what it might be made of. See how thick it is and what the surface looks and feels like. Remember that it can fend off any nasty words a bully may throw at you. Try to see the words landing on the shield and then bouncing back towards the bully.

Pretending that they have a shield which can bounce any name-calling or bad language back to the person who sent it brings two benefits. Firstly they learn to cope better. Next, the bullies usually notice an increase in confidence that comes with visualising a bully shield, and are more likely to seek an easier, more wimpy-looking victim. Kids do need to understand what the shield is for, however. They will still hear a bully being nasty to them but the words will bounce off the repelling shield, finding their way back to the bully.

It can be helpful to spend some time drawing exactly what the shield looks like, as this makes the bully shield fun. Some kids like to use collage or add extra pretend features like bully stun guns to the shield. Drawing and designing the shield is a great time to let the imagination run free and for kids to feel a sense of control over the bullying.

Once kids are happy with the shield design, spend some time practising the visualisation technique. Before bedtime, when they are relaxed, or after exercise are both good times to do this. Get them to close their eyes and settle down to feel calm and quiet. Then imagine where the shield will be on their body. Is it held in front or does it fit all around their body? Will they tie it into place, or does it have straps and buckles? Ask what it feels like. Do they notice its weight? Can they imagine running their hands over the textured surface? Once they have become

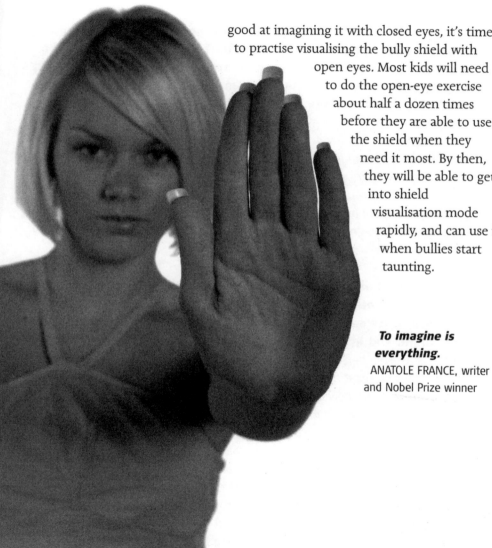

good at imagining it with closed eyes, it's time to practise visualising the bully shield with open eyes. Most kids will need to do the open-eye exercise about half a dozen times before they are able to use the shield when they need it most. By then, they will be able to get into shield visualisation mode rapidly, and can use it when bullies start taunting.

To imagine is everything.
ANATOLE FRANCE, writer and Nobel Prize winner

Defining idea...

How did it go?

Q **I'm a teacher and we've used the bully shield idea in class and several children have found it helpful. There's one little girl who just can't get into it, though. She's into very girlie things, and likes to play with dolls and fairies. Her imagination can be lively, but I think the shield analogy is just too boyish for her. What do you suggest?**

A *It's fantastic she's got a good imagination. Visualisation is great for kids like her. Instead of imagining she has a shield, why not get her to visualise that she has special fairy spells? She might like to visualise a magic wand that she could use to zap any bully who comes near her. The wand might have all sorts of special powers, like preventing any of the bullies' words from causing any damage or even sending them to another country where they can't bother her.*

Q **My son would like to use a bully shield and has drawn a very intricate one, but when it comes to the crunch, he just can't visualise it. He says that when the bullies pick on him, his mind goes blank and he can't think. Why does this happen?**

A *It sounds as if he gets understandably stressed and anxious when he is bullied and that this makes it hard to think. When he – or anyone – is stressed like that, it's hard to try new skills. What he needs is to be able to visualise the shield on autopilot, without thinking, so that it's as natural as breathing. The only way to do this is by practising. At the moment, he's doing the equivalent of trying to cycle away from the bullies without having previously mastered a bike, so it's hardly surprising he's getting stuck. I suggest he practises visualising with his eyes open for a couple of weeks, and then with eyes closed, and in different settings like the swimming pool, supermarket and so on, so that he gets into the habit of doing it automatically. It will then be easier for him to click into shield mode when he needs to.*

27

Believe in yourself

It's hard to believe in yourself when you're continually told you suck or that you're a loser. These techniques help immunise you against the long-term effects of bullying.

The things we believe about ourselves affect almost every aspect of our lives, from our success in the classroom and beyond to how attractive we seem to others.

Bullies can damage what we believe, but this damage is reversible.

Back in the 1960s two researchers, Robert Rosenthal and Lenore Jacobson, gave all the children in an elementary class a test and told teachers that some of children were unusually clever (though they were actually average). They came back at the end of the school year and tested the same class again. Guess what? The children singled out had improved their scores far more than other children. The labels given to kids matter, and other people's perception of them matters too.

You know that expression, mud sticks? I think of the abuse that bullies throw at people like a sort of sticky mud, and unfortunately that sticks too. People who are bullied repeatedly can start to believe things about themselves that are not true. If someone says you are ugly repeatedly, chances are that it will stick, and you might start to believe it yourself.

Here's an idea for you...

It's not enough to write positive statements about yourself. You need to be reminded often. I suggest you write some of your 'I' statements on sticky notes or index cards and put them in places you will look often. How about the inside of your school locker, inside your lunchbox, your bedroom mirror and inside your school bag? Seeing a message like 'I am gorgeous and successful' several times a day will help you believe it and will neutralise the words a bully throws at you. Make sure, however, that your tormentor doesn't see the note. Keep it private.

If others don't intervene in bullying, you might start thinking that you're not worth looking out for and, over time, this belief can stick too. People who are repeatedly bullied start to form vivid images in their mind and start seeing themselves as bullies have described them, not as they really are. It's almost as if bullies have put fairground distorting mirrors into their victims' minds, so that they see their faces, body size and dress sense in the way that the bully described, not the way it really is. This can influence how people present themselves to others. For instance, Joe, who is tall but certainly no giant, was repeatedly teased and called 'lofty' and 'high and mighty' by his tormentors. As a young adult, he walked with a stoop, even years after the bullying had stopped, appearing nervous and unconfident. He had taken in and continued to believe that it would be better if he looked shorter, and came across as timid.

The long-term effects of bullying and damaged self-belief have other serious implications. These include being unable to see yourself as a successful person, being too rigid and afraid of change, and lacking trust in people who genuinely have your best interests at heart. These effects can also mean being too dependent on what other people think of you and having a tendency to see everything in a pessimistic light. Finally, bullying can lead to serious mental-health problems including depression and anxiety.

The good news is that there are several steps you can take to prevent bullying sticking in the first place, and also reversing the effects of any long-term bullying that may have already occurred.

Use 'I' statements

'I' statements are powerful one-liners:

- I am confident.
- I am beautiful.
- I am strong.
- I am resilient.
- I am well organised.
- I am a good student.

Once you've got the hang of statements describing what you are, you can move on to writing some statements about what you can do and what you hope to do.

Here are some example 'I can' statements to get you underway:

- I can beat bullies.
- I can achieve my dreams.
- I can complete this school year.

The third type of affirming statement is 'I will' statements. These help you describe and define a future that is different from that defined by bullies. For instance, bullying can make you feel as if you'll never succeed, or are destined to be a loser. Instead, try writing some statements of what you will do, like this:

- I will lose weight.
- I will have a good day at school today.
- I will go to university.
- I will go to Jenna's party.

Someone's opinion of you does not have to become your reality.

LES BROWN, author of *Live Your Dreams*

Defining idea...

Self-confidence is the first requisite to great undertakings.

SAMUEL JOHNSON

Defining idea...

117

How did it go?

Q **I'd love to have a good day at school, but don't see how writing 'I'll have a great day at school' and sticking this on my mirror is going to magically make everything OK. Can you explain a bit more?**

A *I can understand your scepticism. The principle of self-fulfilling prophecy is that you get what you expect. If you expect a good day, you will be more likely to do things to make that happen – for instance, standing tall in the playground, walking away confidently from bullies, speaking back in a loud voice rather than a timid one and so on. On the other hand, when you expect a bad day, you are more likely to do lots of little things and act in a way that makes that happen. You might – even without thinking about it – give little non-verbal signals to bullies that makes them act differently towards you, bringing about the bad day you expected.*

Q **It's hard coming up with 'I' statements because I can't think of anything good about myself. What do you recommend?**

A *Oh dear, it does sound as if your confidence has had a bashing. It's often difficult to come up with these when you are feeling battered by relentless bullying. A great way to come up with a list is to ask family and friends what they like and value about you. Ask them about your talents and strengths and you should be able to come up with plenty.*

28

Mentoring

Having someone to look up to can change your attitude to being bullied and turbocharge your bully-busting efforts.

Mentors are usually role models, but good mentoring is more than just being a perceptive listener.

There are essentially two types of mentoring that can be helpful in the fight against bullies. The first is receiving mentoring from an adult, and the second is peer mentoring.

Adult mentors

Adult mentors can have all sorts of great effects on your confidence and sense of self-worth. Here are a few examples.

Young people at Central Foundation Girls' School in Tower Hamlets in the UK have seen great results after taking part in a scheme in which Muslims with successful careers mentor children. The girls were teamed up with businesswoman and mentor Noreen Mirza. Noreen regularly took time out from her jewellery business to help the young people design and sell jewellery. They in turn donated profits to the Muslim Youth Helpline.

Here's an idea for you...

Finding an adult mentor needn't be daunting. First decide what you need from a mentor to help you deal with bullies. It might be confidence, self-defence skills or just someone who listens. Next look for a role model who has the qualities you're after. If there's someone you admire, be brave and ask them to be your mentor. Chances are they'll be flattered and say yes. Finally, try not to take it personally if your first-choice mentor says no.

Common experience can be a powerful bond in mentoring relationships, as Toni Mascolo discovered. Toni is one of four Mascolo brothers who own and run the highly successful Toni and Guy hair salons. He found a mentor in an inspirational teacher when he was just fifteen. 'Benedetto Viccari was a strange character, like someone from *Punch* magazine,' he recalls. 'He related to me a lot. He was fifteen himself when he came here, and within five minutes he was discussing things like I was a grown-up man.'

James Dyson, one of the United Kingdom's most prosperous businessmen and inventor of the bestselling eponymous vacuum cleaner, attributes much of his success to his teacher Anthony Hunt. 'We first met in the late 60s while I was an architecture student at the Royal College of Art. He'd been involved in early Foster Rogers' buildings. What Tony gave me was a logical approach to a problem; you break it down into components that you can analyse and sort them out one at a time.'

Blockbuster novelist Tony Parsons recalls the wide ranging influence of his mentor. 'In 1976, Nick Logan was editor of *New Musical Express*. He was the first person who felt like an ally. It was the age of Johnny Rotten; bad behaviour was encouraged. He talked in a way my parents couldn't have and coached me to be like him. Because of him, I'm much more moderate. I haven't taken drugs for a quarter of a century, barely drink and try to stay really fit.'

Peer-mentor schemes

Peer mentoring is a pupil-mentoring scheme designed specifically to tackle bullying and keep kids safe in school. Unlike teachers and parents, peer mentors speak the same language as you do and are more likely to see the world in similar ways.

It's a key part of developing an ability to instigate good relationships and respect for the differences between people. Children are encouraged to report bullying to elected older pupils, the peer mentors. Peer mentors are well respected by their peers, and are chosen because they are felt to be good role models for younger children. If you're looking for someone to confide in, it's often easier to approach a peer mentor than to talk to an adult. In some schools, peer mentors wear badges so it is easy for people to know who they are. Many schools train them in conflict resolution or mediation skills. Most peer-mentoring schemes lead to an increased sense of confidence in mentors as well as mentees. It also increases opportunities for young people to learn about their actions and the effects they might have on others.

Peer-mentoring schemes do require adult supervision. Those taking part are taught by experts to resolve conflict, offer support and advice, help pupils in making friends and on feeding back information about bullying to teachers. However, they're not a substitute for discipline from staff and it's important that young people are not left to deal with serious problems, or that they perceive they have responsibilities beyond their remit. Regular meetings between peer mentors and a supervisor are important to keep this in check.

Mentoring does work in that we've had less bullying in the college since we started. This work needs to be put into practice in other schools.
RACHEL FULLEGAR, Budmouth Technology College student who successfully overcame bullying and, together with two friends, set up a peer-mentoring scheme

Defining idea...

121

How did it go?

Q   I'm on our school council and we've just started a peer-mentoring scheme. A lot of thought and effort has gone into selecting possible mentors, and they have been trained in listening skills by the Samaritans. We're ready to go, but not sure how to encourage kids to take up the scheme without feeling needy or geeky. Any ideas?

A   *The trick is to embed peer mentoring into the fabric of school life. It should be mentioned in the school prospectus, website and newsletter, and make it easy for kids to approach mentors without drawing undue attention to themselves, for instance having a mentor in the library or on playground duty so they are easily accessible.*

Q   We are thinking about suggesting a peer-mentoring scheme in our secondary school. How well do they work?

A   *Schools using peer-mentoring schemes report substantial falls in aggressive behaviour with up to 85% of disputes solved, according to the NSPCC – this charity runs the scheme for the UK Department for Education and Skills. It's certainly worth trying it out.*

29

Random acts of kindness

Bullying is unkind. This idea helps you counteract that nastiness with random acts of kindness.

Kind acts boost morale. But random acts of kindness do much more than that. They help build strong, positive schools and communities where bullies find it hard to flourish.

In the US, a fourteen-year-old girl was quoted in a newspaper about the years of bullying she had endured. Two teenagers were inspired to write letters supporting her, and started a supportive letter-writing campaign. Thousands of letters arrived, from people as young as five and as old as ninety-seven. Letters came from as far away as Japan and Australia and as close as the victim's own town. These strangers' acts of kindness helped her overcome the effects of bullying. Two other kids in Nova Scotia helped a young person who had been bullied for wearing a pink shirt by also wearing pink shirts in solidarity.

It's official. Being kind is good. Ask Dr Allan Luks, former executive director of the Institute for the Advancement of Health and author of the book *The Healing Power of Doing Good*. He surveyed over 3000 volunteers, asking about how they felt when they did a kind act. He found that those who helped others had better health. 'Helping contributes to the maintenance of good health, and it can diminish the effect of

Here's an idea for you...

Why not get together with a crew of your schoolmates and bake biscuits for all the staff at your school? Not just the teachers, but all secretarial staff, canteen workers, cafeteria and administrative employees, as well as health personnel and teacher aides. School staff love surprises as much as the next person. They won't be expecting to be presented with home-made biscuits, and you will be amazed how long the positive effects last. Don't worry about what the bullies might think – they won't be able to pick on you all.

diseases and disorders both serious and minor, psychological and physical,' he said.

When asked how they felt when they did something nice for someone else, 95% of the people involved said they felt 'a rush of euphoria' and then a sense of calm, inner peace and self-worth for hours – or even days – after doing something for someone else. Being connected to feelings of kindness and fair play changes your view of the world, making it seem a fairer and better place. This is the opposite of how the world feels to those who are being bullied.

Kindness has many benefits. Here are some important ones:
- It reverses feelings of depression, hostility, isolation and helplessness;
- It enhances feelings of joy, self-worth, emotional resilience and optimism;
- It decreases the awareness and the intensity of physical pain; and
- It supports the immune system.

So, being kind not only helps mitigate the effects of bullying, it might just help you live longer too. There will be people who are still unconvinced, and I'd like to introduce you to the concept of random acts of kindness.

In 1995, the not-for-profit organisation Random Acts of Kindness was set up. This foundation aims to inspire people to do kind things, just because, without any special reason or ulterior motivation. They're privately funded, not religiously affiliated and all-round good guys. My belief is that their work can counteract a lot of the pessimism and meanness that prevails in so-called progressive society and allows bullies to thrive.

By being kind, I was rewarded with hugs, new friends, and the feeling a person gets when they give for no reason.

JEFF, high school student, Kansas

Defining idea...

Here are some acts of kindness other people have done when inspired by the programme. You don't have to do any or all of them, but I hope they inspire you to do something kind for someone – just because.

- Give someone a hug.
- Leave a note for someone who you appreciate, telling them why.
- Do someone else's household chores for a week, as well as your own.
- Make bird feeders to hang outside the windows of a hospice.
- Tell someone why they are important to you.
- Collect new and used books to donate to a children's ward.
- Volunteer at an animal shelter.
- Make holiday gifts for residents of an assisted-living centre. Visit the centre and present the gifts.
- Offer to clean someone's car.
- Create and post care packages to military personnel.
- Find a small outreach programme in a more distant area, and collect food or supplies for it.
- Collect coats for a women's shelter.
- Share something from your garden.
- Remove noxious weeds from a national park, with the warden's assistance.

For beautiful lips, speak kind words.

AUDREY HEPBURN

Defining idea...

- Help a food bank sort food.
- Clean, paint, and organise space for after-school programmes.
- Walk someone else's dog for them.

Many – but not all – bullies have been bullied themselves. It's no excuse, but some bullying seems to be contagious. Kindness is also contagious. When you do something kind, like paying for the kid in the lunch queue behind you as well as for your own lunch, the recipient feels like doing something kind too.

How did it go?

Q   I've been bullied for months and don't feel at all like being kind. How can I get into it?

A   *The great thing about random acts of kindness is that you don't have to feel kind to do them. In fact, the reverse is true. The more kind things you do, the more kind you'll feel.*

Q   I think of kind things I might do but then worry that I'm being overbearing or getting under people's feet. How can I know when kind actions are truly welcome?

A   *The first thing to do is relax. If you are feeling anxious and eager to please, being a randomly kind person can feel like an awkward endeavour. Chill out a little and it should flow more naturally.*

30

Bully box

Sometimes kids want to tell someone about a bully, but don't want to risk making it worse. A bully box helps them report bullying without having to mention names.

Bully boxes can alert teachers to a bullying problem, without kids having to work up the courage to speak out, or risk being victimised for doing so.

A bully box is a way of telling teachers about a bullying problem safely and anonymously. I first came across bully boxes when I was working as a child psychiatrist in the county of Kent in the UK. I was impressed as they seemed to be an extremely effective way of getting on top of problems before they were exacerbated.

In essence, a bully box is a secure way for kids to report any bullying they may have experienced or witnessed. All you need to get started is a big cardboard box, sealed and with a slot cut in the top, which is put somewhere safe and accessible. Anyone who is being bullied or who knows about a bully's activities can write it down – completely anonymously – and post it in the bully box. This is a neat way for children to let adults know about bullies without having to speak out or name names in public.

Here's an idea for you...

Why not use a bully box for a trial period, say a term? Once teachers have discovered where and when the bullies strike, the whole school could work to identify those times when bullying doesn't happen. Everyone could spend more time in the parts of school that are safer, and bullies are more likely to know that their actions will no longer go unnoticed or unreported. Kids whose names show up frequently in the bully box could be watched more closely by teachers.

Different adults have different approaches to this idea. Some make the point that they are unable to take action unless people give their names and the name of the bully, as otherwise the bully box is just hearsay and rumour. However, schools who have used anonymous bully boxes find that teachers are generally more aware of bullying.

A bully box is also a good way of alerting teachers to bullying hot spots, even without any names being associated with the bullying going on there. There are often a few areas – for instance, a nook in the playground behind a wall or a secluded place indoors like the cloakrooms – where bullies lurk and where bullying is, therefore, more likely to take place. If teachers are aware of the hot spots, they can arrange to keep an eye on these particular places and hopefully deter further bullying. A bully box can help cultivate an attitude of vigilance.

As a minimum, those using a bully box ought to be recording what has happened, who witnessed it and when it took place. Any further details, like the names of the people involved and the names of the bullies themselves, can help teachers take appropriate action. Kids will be able to effectively use a bully box if they can trust what happens to the information left there, so clear guidelines on confidentiality are invaluable. If children feel that the information they post will be taken seriously, then they are more likely to report what they experience, see and hear.

If the bully box is effective, you might also like to have a sorry box. This is a box where – you've guessed it – people can leave anonymous apologies for things they have done wrong. Each week the letters saying sorry are emptied out of the sorry box and displayed on a notice board for everyone to read. It's a good way for people who are feeling bad but cowardly to start to make amends for their actions.

A problem shared is a problem halved.
Proverb

Defining idea...

How did it go?

Q **Children might want to put something in the bully box but may be worried about being seen, recognised as a tell-tale and possibly victimised as a consequence. Any idea that can help here?**

A *Well, some schools have a system where kids can hand a letter in to the school office or reception marked 'for the bully box' and a staff member will drop it in for them. There are lots of reasons why someone might have to drop a letter off at the office, after all.*

Q **We've found that bullies are using the bully box to make up stories about other people to try and get them into trouble. There's so much stuff in the boxes, we don't know what's true and what's just been made up for revenge. How can we tell?**

A *It's a real pity that the bullies are using an intervention as yet another way of picking on their classmates. My advice would be to provide a sorry box, to allow those who have done wrong to make amends. I also suggest you take each letter in the bully box seriously, and trust your instincts about the motivations of each writer.*

Q **We tried a bully box and found it very difficult not to end up dwelling on what has gone wrong in our school. Not knowing who the culprits are has been really hard for the staff team; we're sad that bullying behaviour seems to outweigh any good. It's hard to be positive. Should we scrap it?**

A *Firstly, go easy on yourselves. Just making the change and introducing a bully box is a sign of your commitment to doing things differently and looking at school bullying in a new way. Change isn't always easy. One way of remembering the positives is to have a time each week in school to celebrate successes, perhaps by incorporating this into an end-of-week assembly or staff meeting. Hang on in there.*

31

Say it again...

Asking bullies to repeat what they've said is often enough to put them off. They'll often be fazed. Most haven't got the nerve to say it again when you ask them to.

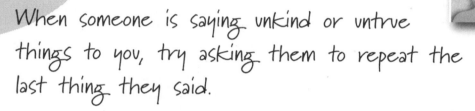

When someone is saying unkind or untrue things to you, try asking them to repeat the last thing they said.

Many bullies use words to hurt or humiliate. They use tactics including name calling, insulting, making racist or sexist remarks, commenting on your appearance and relentless teasing. Many kids find this type of bullying especially hard as it happens quickly; it catches them off-guard and unsure about how to react to it. Often verbal bullies are a bit older, sometimes with a better command of language, or are of the same age but use verbal fluency and their innate articulate ability to intimidate others.

Sometimes asking bullies to repeat what they have said can put them off. Often even the most articulate verbal bully isn't brave enough to repeat what's been said so it gets toned down. If they repeat it, you've made them do something they hadn't planned on, and this gives you some control. Asking bullies to repeat taunts or insults usually takes the wind out of their sails.

Here's an idea for you...

You can use this technique by pretending that you have a scratched CD inside you that keeps jumping on one track. When a bully says something insulting or offensive, just keep repeating, over and over, 'can you say that again?' Then walk off with confidence when you get your answer.

An effective retort to verbal bullying is to ask bullies to 'say it again'. Most verbal bullies, that is the ones who tease, taunt and talk about you, are cowardly. They lack the courage to repeat an insult in the same way and are more likely to modify it. Keep asking a bully to 'say it again' and chances are that they will repeat the insult, but it will be less offensive. It's hard to say something in exactly the same way a second time, and bullies are likely to be quite surprised when you ask them to repeat themselves. Catching them off their guard like this means they are more likely to tone an insult down.

Here's an example. Say a bully was insulting John's mother and calling her a slag, here's how he could respond:

Bully: 'Your mum's a slag.'

John: 'I didn't hear you, can you say it again?'

Bully: 'Yeah, your mum, she's, you know, she's a bit of a slag.'

John: 'Can you say that again?'

Bully: 'Say what again?'

John: 'What you said about my mum.'

Bully: 'You heard me.'

John: 'I'm sorry, I didn't hear what you said about her. Could you say it again?'

Bully: 'I didn't say anything about your mum.'

Putting it into practice

There are several ways you could ask a bully to say it again. But firstly, it's important not to sound argumentative or antagonistic when you ask for repetition. When using the 'say it again' technique, use a neutral tone of voice, asking the bully as if you were genuinely curious. As soon as you start to look upset or wound up, a bully will realise he or she can get a rise from you and is more likely to continue being mean. Here are some ways you might ask:

Repetition does not transform a lie into a truth.
FRANKLIN D. ROOSEVELT

Defining idea...

- What did you say?
- What was that?
- I didn't hear what you said, can you repeat it?
- I couldn't make that out, would you say it again?

By being like John and asking the bully to repeat the insult, you gain control of his bullying. When a bully insults you, he is throwing the taunt at you. Asking him to repeat it is the verbal equivalent of you picking up the taunt and throwing it back to him. He won't expect it to come back, so has to think quickly, under pressure. Often, this makes a bully reflect on the nastiness of what's been said, and then feel bad about it. It's likely that the bully will feel uncomfortable or ashamed of what's been said, so what usually happens is that they offer you a weaker version of their original insult – just like the bully did to John in the example.

A graceful taunt is worth a thousand insults.
LOUIS NIZER, American trial lawyer

Defining idea...

135

How did it go?

Q There are some bullies at the end of my road and every day they call me a wanker. I asked these bullies to 'say it again' and they did. They called me a wanker over and over again. I tried to be really neutral and didn't get cross. What went wrong?

A *Nothing. You've been unlucky. When bullies work in a pack, they often feel more bravado in front of each other, so sometimes this idea doesn't work as well as when you use it on an individual bully. If this happens again, stay just as calm and neutral as you have been, but instead of 'say it again', say quite casually, 'yes, you told me that yesterday. I heard you yesterday'. You can still use the scratched CD technique in this idea; just say 'I heard you already' instead of 'say it again'.*

Q I've tried this, and although the girl who's bullying me tones it down, she still says horrible things. What can I do?

A *When she does this, have a rejoinder ready for the weaker version of the insult. For instance, 'wow, I didn't think someone like you would have said something like that, so I assumed I'd misheard you,' or perhaps even 'I really hope you feel better for having said that'.*

32

Calming rhythms

Those ancient Greeks were on to something. Apollo, god of sun and light, was also god of medicine and music.

In Francis Bacon's words, 'the poets did well to conjoin music and medicine in Apollo, because the office of medicine is but to tune this curious harp of man's body, and to reduce it to harmony.'

Singing, listening or moving to music and playing instruments can all help soothe children battered by bullying. Researchers have shown that tempo affects levels of excitement and mode affects mood. When music was played to children and young people in a major key, they were more likely to have happy moods, but when the same music was played in a minor key, they more often felt sad.

Children often find it hard to express emotion when they have been bullied. It's healthy and normal to experience a wide range of feelings in those circumstances, from numbness to despair and a desire for revenge, but for young people these feelings are often overwhelming. Percussion instruments like drums, maracas, bells – basically anything that you thump or shake – can, in particular, help children express some of the anger and frustration that bullying often stirs up. Don't worry if

Here's an idea for you... **Make a home music station by keeping some maracas or a tambourine by your CD player at home, together with a selection of styles of music. When your kids come home after a bad day with the bullies, encourage them to go to the music station and play, shake, beat or sing it out until it feels better.**

you haven't got a drum kit lying around the house. Empty paint tins, saucepans and upturned buckets are all good stand-ins.

Music can help bullied kids in various ways. Drumming helps them express ideas and feelings, for starters. Social skills are enhanced through listening to others and working with them, and it can therefore help reduce behavioural problems. There are some less obvious benefits, too. Music also increases endorphin levels, dulling pain and creating a warm feeling of well-being, while self-esteem grows through striving to achieve goals. Tenacity is achieved through the discipline of regular practice sessions.

Problem-solving skills develop by experimenting with and exploring the rhythmic patterns of music, too. And music can enable kids to get across any painful or complex feelings, perhaps more easily than using words. It offers a means of expression to shy or frightened children who find it hard to speak about their experiences and emotions. Converting negative feelings like anger and sadness into musical expression is empowering. Finally, singing songs can also help the brain make new connections, and so may stimulate new ideas for coping with many situations, including bullying. Whenever a growing brain is stimulated, either new connections are made or existing ones are strengthened.

You don't have to buy a grand piano to help your child reap these benefits; there are many ways to get involved in music. Keep a radio on in the house, consider an after-school music group, encourage singing and allow kids to express themselves using musical instruments, improvised or not, or their voices. Younger kids will also enjoy using percussion instruments, and all children can explore ways of making sounds to express different feelings like anger or sadness.

Once kids are older, encourage them to notice what music they like to listen to when they're angry or upset. Many people instinctively select the right type of music to soothe their mood, and it's often not what you might expect. For instance, it may not be right for you to listen first to soothing music when you're feeling wound up. Some people find that sort of thing makes them feel even worse and prefer something more up tempo, and sometimes you're better off choosing music that matches your mood rather than the mood you're hoping to get into. The same is true for children, so encourage them to experiment until they discover what really helps.

One of the things we all need is to feel heard and to make connections with others. When a person hits a drum they're immediately transported into the present moment. That's good for stress levels. In the present moment, it's very difficult to be stressed.
ROBERT LAWRENCE FRIEDMAN, psychotherapist and drum circle facilitator

Defining idea...

Opera is when a guy gets stabbed in the back and instead of bleeding he sings.
ED GARDNER, American comic actor, writer and director

Defining idea...

139

How did it go?

Q **My daughter isn't good at expressing her feelings verbally and I've wondered if music might help. We're not sure if she's musically inclined, though, and I don't want to waste a lot of money on an instrument in case she isn't. Any way of knowing?**

A *The first thing to say is that you don't have to have any special musical ability to enjoy music or use this idea. You also don't need to cough up a lot of money for an instrument. Children can play glass jam jars filled with water or shake a tin with gravel in it. If you do decide to pursue formal music tuition, many shops allow you to hire an instrument before committing to a large purchase.*

Q **My daughter is great at the violin and practises often. It seems to help her when she is fed up after being bullied. She derives a sense of achievement from it, but I worry as she does this on her own and it doesn't give her a chance to really make any friends. I've suggested finding someone to play duets with but she isn't keen. Any ideas?**

A *Why not get her to join a youth orchestra? She is likely to meet like-minded musical friends and will develop team-playing skills that can help her combat bullying too. Children in youth orchestras develop good self-expression and self-worth, which are just as important skills in life as they are in coping with bullies.*

33

Booked

Many people who've been bullied have been helped by keeping a diary.

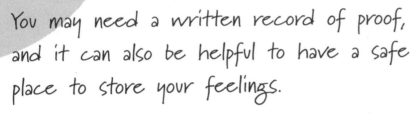
You may need a written record of proof, and it can also be helpful to have a safe place to store your feelings.

Having a written record of bullying is incredibly important when bringing bullies to task. A bullying diary has two functions. It provides a written record that can be shared with helping adults including teachers, police and lawyers, and also helps you make sense of your feelings.

Some people find it helpful to keep separate diaries, one for recording facts, and one for feelings, but I think that as long as you understand the different purposes, you could record the information in the same place.

You might want to use a sheet marked like the one on the next page this for keeping a factual record.

Try to keep a strictly factual account in this part of the diary. Whether or not you use something like the table, stick to answering these questions:

■ When did the bullying happen?
■ What was said and done?
■ Who was involved?

Date	Time	What happened?	Where did this take place?	Who was involved in bullying?	Who else was there?	Additional notes
27/11/08	8.15am	I was pushed against the wall and was called slag and bitch	On the way to school, just outside the gate	Sammy, George and Ryan	Nikki and Zane were there but they didn't say anything	George took my hair scrunchie and still has it
29/11/08	1.25pm	I was stopped from getting to the water fountain at break time	In the corridor between the art room and homeroom	George, Ryan and Zane	Mellissa was with me and she was telling them to stop it	I was trying to fill my water bottle but the boys took it and were throwing it. When I got it back they stood in front of the water fountain so I couldn't get a drink

- Where did it take place?
- Was anything taken?
- Who else was there?
- What did the bystanders say or do?

If you don't know the names of the people who bullied you, write as detailed a description as you can. These prompts may help you:

- Was it a boy or a girl?
- How old did they look?
- What race were they?
- How tall were they?
- What colour hair did they have?
- What sort of hairstyle?
- What were they wearing?

How about:

- What was on their head: cap, beanie, hoodie?
- Did anything have a distinctive logo?
- What was on their feet: trainers, boots, flip-flops?
- Were they wearing glasses or sunnies?
- Any tattoos, jewellery or piercings?

Once you have completed your factual records, use a fresh page to write about your feelings. You might or might not want to share the feelings pages with other people. It's up to you. The advantage of keeping feelings and facts on separate pages is that you can photocopy what you need to share, while still keeping personal stuff completely personal.

Here's an idea for you...

A fine-looking notebook can be a great place to record your feelings. You could either select something ready made or decorate it yourself with stickers or drawings. If you're feeling stuck, try writing a letter to yourself. Alternatively, you could ask yourself, 'how am I feeling right now?' Some people find it helpful to have a special place to write, perhaps relaxing on a beanbag or at a special table in the sun. Playing your favourite music can also help your mind associate writing your feelings down with feeling better.

Defining idea...

I never travel without my diary. One should always have something sensational to read in the train.
OSCAR WILDE

You might like to use these three questions to help you write this part:

- How did you feel during the bullying?
- How do you feel now?
- What needs to happen for you to feel better?

Only write about feelings when you want to. It's important not to allow writing about your feelings about bullying to become an unpleasant task. It's easy to feel down on yourself over bullying, so it's especially important to cut yourself some slack over diary writing. Most people miss a few days or even weeks of writing. If that happens, don't fret, just write about feelings next time you have a chance. After a few months of recording your feelings, you might like to read back over what you've written. Many people find they can learn from what they have written. You might notice certain things you do that help you feel better, and could plan to do more of them, for instance.

How did it go?

Q Isn't it potentially unhelpful to spend so long dwelling on bullying by writing about it?

A *I can see why you might think that, but research has shown that writing reduces unpleasant thoughts about negative events like bullying and improves your working memory. These improvements, researchers believe, may free up brain space for other tasks, including the ability to cope effectively with stress.*

Q I'd like to learn more about writing a diary. What can you suggest?

A *You might like to read some diaries like* The Diary of a Young Girl *by Anne Frank,* Zlata's Diary: A Child's Life in Wartime Sarajevo *by Zlata Filipovic or* Alice, I Think *by Susan Juby. All three contain a candid combination of facts and feelings.*

34

Cool down

Some kids become very hot-tempered when they're bullied. Angry, aggressive outbursts invariably make bullying worse.

Coping with angry feelings is an important part of coping with bullies.

Acting in an angry manner has got a bad name. Kids who have a reputation for being angry are rarely popular and are often generally avoided. Yet anger is a remarkably useful emotion and, if channelled properly, is one of the most effective ways of addressing injustice. Feeling angry about something can give people the energy and focus to make meaningful changes and do things they are not able to do when they are cool and collected. But it's important to be clear about what's acceptable and what's not.

Frightening others, shouting rudely or smashing property are actions. They, and other things like them, are not OK. Learning to control actions that may follow feelings of anger is important. Feeling angry when being bullied is normal and understandable, but getting violent will only make things worse. If kids can keep their cool and avoid being drawn into a heated dispute or fight, bullies become losers. They can't control their victims any longer.

Here's an idea for you...

Children appreciate it if you suggest a few ways to let anger out safely, so here are some:

- ■ **Hitting a large cushion with a rolled-up newspaper.**
- ■ **Pushing hard against the wall with flat palms.**
- ■ **Screwing up old newspaper.**
- ■ **Scribbling with crayons.**
- ■ **Tearing up pages from an old phone book.**
- ■ **Running to the end of the road or garden and back, as fast as possible.**
- ■ **Stamping feet loudly outside.**

During an angry episode many different things are going on, from actions, thoughts and feelings to the way we communicate that anger to other people and the effect it has on them. We can't always control our thoughts or feelings, but we can control our actions and the way we communicate our anger to those around us. This can seriously lessen the effect of our anger on others.

Next time your child gets really angry, wait until he has calmed down. Then talk to him and see if you can encourage him to explain just why he felt like he did. Explain that you want to understand what was going on so you can help. Before children can express anger, they need a range of words to describe how they feel. Many kids display aggression because they simply don't know how to express their frustrations in any other way. They need an appropriate vocabulary to convey what's going wrong and you can help your child develop one. See how many words you can come up with to describe feeling really angry and hide them in a word search grid. Here are some suggestions to start with (you'll need to adapt the words to the age of your child, of course): upset, cross, crazy, temper, wild, storm, explosion, snarling, snappy, crabby, frustrated, rage, irritated, livid, annoyed, furious, berserk…

Every single one of us has our own little signs that alert us to the fact that we're about to lose it. Explain to children that the trick to controlling anger is being able to identify their own personal anger warning signs, and help them to recognise them. Here's an example: 'My cheeks get hot and I know I'm going red. I talk louder. I clench my fists. I can feel my heart beating quickly and my mouth gets dry.' Once kids are aware of their own signs, you can start pointing them out: 'Looks like you're starting to feel out of control. Do you feel yourself starting to get angry?' The more you can help your child identify those early warning signs when his anger is first triggered, the more likely that he'll be to calm down.

Anger is a momentary madness, so control your passion or it will control you.
HORACE

Defining idea...

If it's hard for children to control their temper when they're being bullied, you can help by encouraging them to start keeping a record sheet of what happens. It would look something like this:

The target for my anger was: Jacob Morris.
The situation was: He was trying to steal my bag.
The thought I had was: He can't have my bag, I hate him.
The amount of my anger was (mark a cross on the scale in the right place):

0————————5————X————10

  not at all angry   the angriest I've ever felt

What I did: I kicked Jacob, threw his book across the playground
What happened because of what I did? I got a detention and mum cried
How did I feel? Really sad
What could I do differently? Walked away, told a teacher he had my bag.

147

How did it go?

Q **My son has been bullied over the past year. The bullying stopped once we found out about it but he now flies off the handle really easily and sometimes seems like a little bully himself, especially with his younger sister. How can I help?**

A *Unfortunately many kids are left with a legacy of anger after experiencing bullying which has left them feeling powerless. The first step you can take is to keep a record of when he loses control. When he's feeling calmer, try to gently explore what the triggers were. Ask him what happened and what he was thinking. It's highly likely that he's jumping to conclusions or making assumptions. He may also be stressed by something else in school or at home. An open approach in which he feels able to express himself without violence is the best way forward.*

Q **My daughter knows the theory, but when she is confronted that all goes out of the window and I'm sure she provokes bullies by giving vent to her anger. What can she do?**

A *Before facing the bullies, encourage her to do a deal with herself to stay cool. When she feels herself getting hot and red, get her to visualise a red traffic light, prompting her to stop and think before going with the angry feeling.*

35
Touch and go

Has your child been pushed around, kicked or shoved? This hands-on idea is a fail-safe route to helping them feel better.

Touch is the first sense we develop. Bullying is one of the worst sorts of touches, but gentle touches can repair those wrongs.

Pushing, punching, kicking or that awful 'accidentally on purpose' knocking, are the sorts of touches bullies often favour. This latter one, in particular, is a cowardly way of inflicting pain or causing humiliation while making it look like an accident to a casual observer. But you can counteract the effects of nasty touches like that – by using massage.

Research has shown that children who are massaged show decreased levels of stress hormones. At the Skönberga school in southern Sweden, massage is part of the curriculum and has been found to be a powerful anti-bullying measure. Children can be massaged by teachers but also learn to massage each other. The school has found that empathy, co-operation and responsibility have increased. Having a slow massage is an excellent way to improve your quality of life, whatever your age. In the present climate, however, responsible teachers ought to ensure that a school policy on massage is in place, and that there is signed, informed consent from parents about this intervention. A minority of teachers have abused parental trust

Here's an idea for you...

Massage your forehead and you feel stress melting away, so teach children how to do this for those days when they've had a bad time with the bullies. First, cosy up in a comfortable chair. Now put the fingertips of your right hand on your right eyebrow. Pressing quite hard, slide your fingertips along the eyebrow until you reach your temple. Massage your temple by making small circles with your fingertips. Finally repeat using your left hand on your left eyebrow. If you can, spend a few minutes sitting quietly with your eyes closed. That should help.

but it would be a great pity if any backlash meant that children missed out on the potential benefits of massage.

If your child is being bullied, here are just some of the ways massage can help:

- It reduces stress and tension;
- It relieves pain;
- It increases levels of serotonin, protecting against depression;
- It increases endorphins, the body's natural pain killers;
- It strengthens the immune system.

Scientists at the Touch Research Institute in Florida have verified that massage plays a role in reducing stress. They split fifty people into two groups. One group had a chair massage twice a week for five weeks while the others were asked to just relax in a chair at the same times. At the end of the five weeks, both groups were less depressed, but only the group who'd been massaged were less stressed as well.

If you want to give your bullied little one a massage, here's how:

1. Warm your hands and put a clean, fluffy towel on the bed.
2. Have him lie face down on his front and gently stroke his back. Stroke up and over his back and along his arms.
3. Gently knead his shoulders.

4. Make a gentle wringing stroke up over his body.
5. Smooth down the spine using alternating hands, starting at the base of his neck and working down to the base of his spine.
6. Bend his knee up and work on one foot at a time.
7. Work around the ankle with your fingertips.
8. Gently clasp the foot between heels of hand and massage, moving both hands in a circular motion.
9. Gently squeeze the heel with one hand and massage up the sole of his foot using the thumbs of your other hand.
10. Massage the toes, gently squeezing, rotating and pulling each one in turn.

Many parents wonder about massage oil, but what's truly important is touch. Unperfumed baby oil is gentle on young skins.

Older children and teenagers will probably not be keen for their parents to massage them. They might prefer to see a professional massage therapist. Aromatherapy massage uses oils applied in long, flowing strokes, called 'effleurage'. These oils can be soothing or invigorating. Swedish massage is much more energetic; it's intended to energise by stimulating your circulation. Feldenkrais, Rolfing and Hellerwork are varieties of deep-tissue massage, which are great for taking strain out of deeper muscles and can help with injuries.

Every child, no matter the age, should be massaged at bedtime on a regular basis.
DR TIFFANY FIELD, Touch Research Institute in Miami

Defining idea...

In the absence of touching and being touched, people of all ages can sicken and grow touch starved.
DIANE ACKERMAN, *in A Natural History of The Senses*

Defining idea...

How did it go?

Q **My six-year-old daughter has been bullied and it has made her very sad. I have tried massaging her but she doesn't stay still. What can I do?**

A *First of all, check she's happy being massaged. Some children don't like it and if she's one of them it's crucial to respect her point of view. Many parents find incorporating massage into evening and bedtime routines is helpful. Children are often in 'wind-down' mode and more amenable to massage. Also, keep in mind that even five minutes of massage can feel like a very long time to a six year old. Other ruses include massaging her while your partner reads her a bedtime story or massaging her in the bath when she's relatively still.*

Q **I don't feel comfortable with the idea of my teenage daughter being massaged by another adult but am not always confident of my technique. Any suggestions?**

A *There are often courses you can go on to learn more about massage techniques. Why not check out what your local adult education college has on offer? Also bear in mind that qualified massage therapists are used to young people feeling nervous and will cover her with drapes and towels. Hand or foot massage or a head and shoulder massage may also be more acceptable to her.*

36

Brain versus brawn

You know the saying, do what you've always done and get what you've always got? It's true. This idea helps kids use their brains to find new solutions to bullying.

Often bullying feels like an intractable problem; it's easy to feel as though everything's been tried. It's time to put all the preconceptions aside, and get brainstorming.

Developing calm, clear thinking and generating creative solutions is a good way to combat bullies' brawn. Check out this four stage problem-solving strategy. It was developed by Professor of Special Education, Carolyn Hughes and has been shown to be effective in many different situations.

Try guiding your child through each of these stages:
1. Problem identification.
2. Make an action plan.
3. Put it into practice.
4. Revise it in the light of experience.

Here's an idea for you...

Children learn problem solving by watching how the adults around them solve their own problems and imitating them. Everyone, whatever their age, encounters bullies, so the next time you run into a potential bully at work, talk about it in front of your kids. Demonstrate your own solution, but be careful. Use a structured problem-solving approach and don't just jump on the first solution. Take all the opportunities you can to show your children how to problem solve.

Problem identification

Help your child get to the roots of the problem by asking these questions:

- What do you want?
- What do you have now?
- What's the gap between what you want and what you have?

Younger kids may struggle with the last question, so you can help by explaining how you see the gap; that should get them going. Once you have agreed on something, make a note of the gap between what your child wants and what your child currently has. This statement ought to define the problem. Here's an example for clarity. 'Harry wants to travel on the school bus without being picked on. Right now, he gets on the bus but other kids say mean things to him, and he cries. He wants to be able to find a way to get to school without being picked on and without crying.'

Make an action plan

Next, you need to consider possible solutions to the problem. There are a number of ways of doing this. You might pick a solution that sounds like it would be good. This is easy – it doesn't require any previous knowledge – but there's no way to know whether such a solution would actually work. Then you could select a solution from a list of options. Unfortunately, not every problem is so straightforward, and every solution would need to be examined to determine the pros and cons. You could also use an analogy from a similar situation to the one your child is in. This can be a quick starting point but analogies are not always relevant and the solutions may not match your child's particular problem. Finally, you could brainstorm to generate a number of potential solutions to the problem. This method of identifying a course of action can be fun. It's probably likely to work best, too.

No problem can stand the assault of sustained thinking.
VOLTAIRE

Defining idea…

When you're brainstorming, give children the freedom to say anything, however daft it seems to you. Don't try and impose your ideas on them, or stamp on anything immediately because it sounds impractical. After each suggestion they come up with, say something like 'yes, you could do that, and what else might you try? What else might work?' This helps them generate as long a list as they can.

Once you have got a list of possible solutions identify the pros and cons of each. Do this by asking, 'what do you think might happen if you did that?' Then get them to think about what they would need for each option, and consider all possible risks and costs. Now you're in a position to review each option and select the one that seems to fit best.

Put it into practice

Now it's time for action. To help children implement their solution smoothly, make sure they really know what the solution is. You might need to role play and have a trial run.

Don't find fault. Find a remedy.
HENRY FORD

Defining idea…

You also need to make sure they have the skills necessary to do the things they described. If new skills are necessary – say your son wants to improve his football so he can fit in with the group – make sure there is a realistic time frame available. Then decide when and how to implement the new solution. The start of term? The beginning of next week?

Revise it in the light of experience

If you've worked your way through the process, the new solution has probably worked well, so take some time to assess things and make any adjustments if you need to. You can run through it again if necessary, of course.

How did it go?

Q   We get stuck doing all of this because my son gets very vengeful and offers solutions that would get him into trouble, like 'beating the bullies to a pulp'. How can I encourage him to think of sensible, workable solutions?

A   By not censoring him at the brainstorming stage. Having these thoughts doesn't mean he will act on them, particularly if you help him think through the pros and cons. Let him think of any possible solution, no matter how outlandish. Then encourage him to think through those advantages and disadvantages. You might end up with something like this. Solution: Beating bullies to a pulp. Pros: I'll feel better. They will be hurt. Cons: I could get expelled or sent to prison. It makes me just as bad as them. They might fight back and hurt me.

Q   We worked through the stages systematically, but it hasn't gone at all as we thought it would. What do we do now?

A   If it didn't go quite to plan, it's time for a review. Start at the beginning, and work through it again, checking as you go. My guess is that either you've not defined the problem accurately (that's quite common) or that your deadlines for getting started have drifted a bit.

37

Dead loss

Every year, schoolchildren take their lives because they can't cope with any more bullying.

Here's how to prevent a child you know becoming a tragic statistic.

The most shocking thing for many adults is that some children would rather kill themselves than be torn apart by more bullying. Thirteen-year-old Sian Yates was found hanging at her home after being bullied for being Welsh. The only Welsh girl at her school in Leicester, the teenager – described by her former head teacher as 'an amazing and popular student' – had been taunted by a jealous classmate.

According to the World Health Organisation, more people are dying from suicide than in all of the armed conflicts around the world and, in many places, about the same or more than those dying from traffic accidents. In all countries, suicide is now one of the three leading causes of death among people between the ages of fifteen and thirty-four.

It's hard to say with certainty how many of these suicides are associated with bullying. The charity Kidscape attempted to explore the link between bullying and suicide in it study 'The long-term effects of bullying'. It established that almost half of the kids it surveyed had contemplated suicide and a fifth had made at least one suicide attempt.

Here's an idea for you...

Many adults just don't know how to talk to kids about suicide. It's not an easy topic to bring up, but avoiding it can literally be a matter of life and death. My suggestion is to keep a calm, open manner, and use questions like these: Many children who are bullied start to feel life is not worth living. Has it ever felt like that for you? What have you thought about? Have you ever tried to do that? What stopped you?

Could your child be depressed?

Many bullied children develop depression, but it can be hard for parents and teachers to distinguish depression from normal teenage mood swings. The following checklist is a guide. The presence or absence of any of these factors doesn't mean a child is or isn't depressed, but the more that hold true, the more inclined you should be to obtain a medical opinion:

- Being irritable or snapping more.
- Loss of interest in hobbies or sports.
- Frequent absences from school.
- Poor academic progress.
- Poor concentration.
- Finding decisions difficult to make.
- Increase or decrease in sexual activity.
- Losing interest in activities which once were fun.
- Changes in eating and sleeping habits.
- Expressing inappropriate guilt.
- Worrying about not being good enough.
- Expressing hopelessness and a sense of having nothing to look forward to.
- Crying easily.
- Expressing suicidal thoughts.

It's also not easy to know if a child or young person may actually be feeling suicidal. These seven suicide warning signs ought to help:

- Talking about suicide, death or dying.
- Withdrawing from friends.
- Experiencing a severe loss, especially a relationship break-up.
- Losing interest in hobbies.
- Giving away valued possessions.
- Increased use of alcohol or drugs.
- Expressing a sense of hopelessness.

Anyone desperate enough for suicide... should be desperate enough to go to creative extremes to solve problems: elope at midnight, stow away on the boat to New Zealand and start over, do what they always wanted to do but were afraid to try.
HERACLITUS

Defining idea...

The last point is perhaps the most powerful predictor of suicide. Evidence of hopelessness has been found in more than 90% of all suicide notes.

If you think your child, or a child in your class, may be suicidal, don't leave them unattended. Call for professional help. A school guidance counsellor, school nurse or GP is a good place to turn, as they will have links with specialist professionals if needed. Make sure all the kids in your care know about confidential telephone helplines, like Childline in the UK.

Suicide is a permanent solution to a temporary problem.
PHIL DONAHUE

Defining idea...

How did it go?

Q **My niece has been bullied at school and gets called 'blonde bimbo' a lot. Recently she took an overdose of paracetamol, but told her mother. She seems OK now, but we're not sure if this was meant to be a serious attempt or just a cry for help. What should we do?**

A *Professor Keith Hawton and his colleagues at the Oxford Centre for Suicide Prevention have identified that this sort of self-harm is common in teenage girls. Some 7%–14% of adolescents will self-harm at some time in their life. Deliberate self-harm ranges from behaviours with no suicidal intent (but with the intent to communicate distress or relieve tension) through to suicide. It is important she is seen by a mental health professional skilled in assessing where she is in this range, and to determine what type of help she needs.*

Q **My son has said that he has sometimes felt he would be better off dead, but that he wouldn't do anything as he wouldn't want to hurt me and his gran. I'm scared to leave him alone now and he says that he wishes he hadn't told me because me watching him all the time is bugging him. Can you help?**

A *Again, I'd like to draw attention to some of Professor Hawton's work. Around 20%–45% of older teenagers report having had suicidal thoughts at some time. Although it is important to watch kids who have active plans to end their lives, it's also important to tease apart the subtle difference between thoughts and plans. It's encouraging that your son can be open with you. My advice would be to take his feelings seriously and obtain professional advice on how to proceed. As long as he has no current plans for suicide, it is worth following his wish to be left alone.*

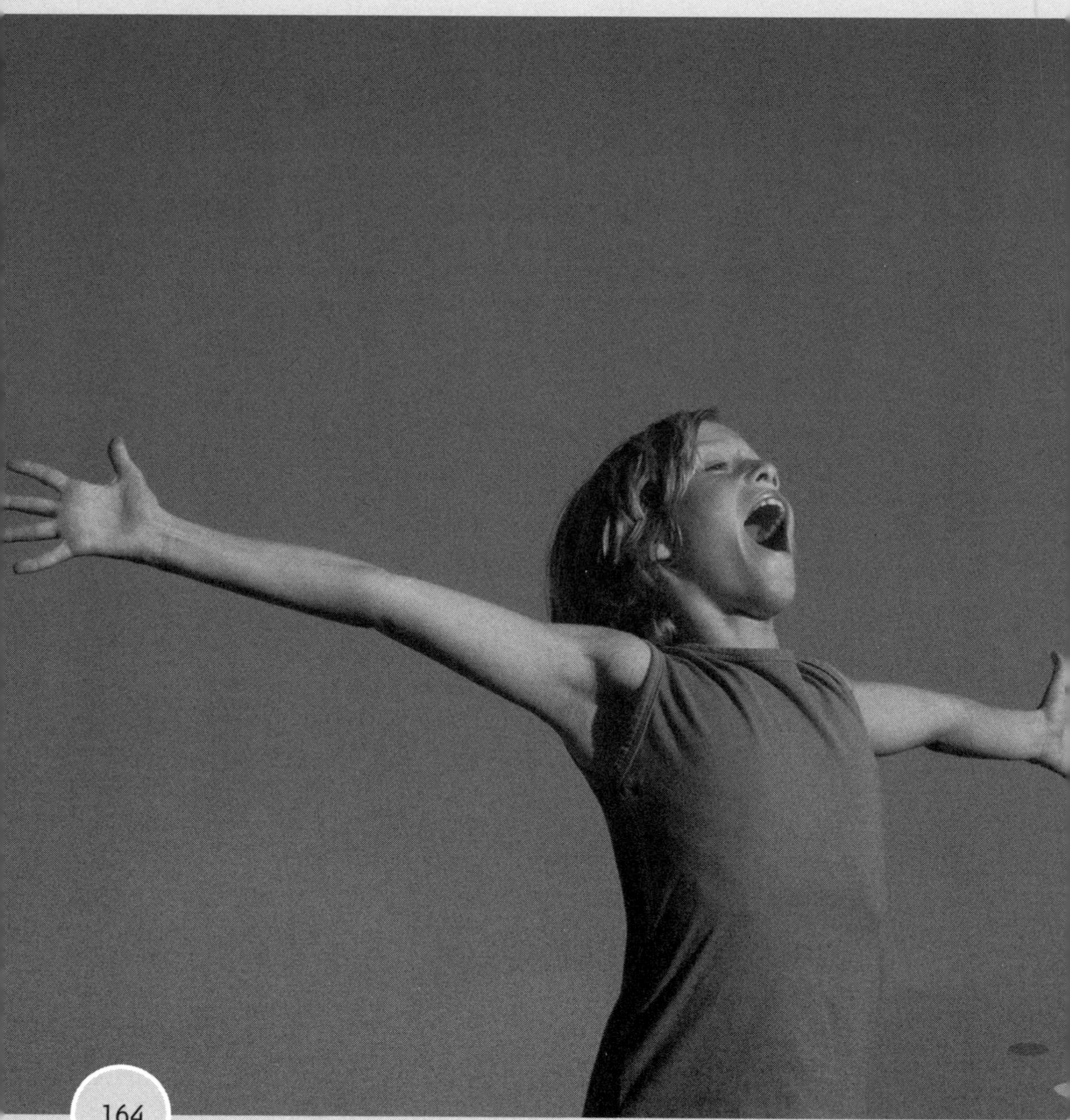

38

Loud and clear

Mumbling or speaking like a squeaky little mouse will mark you out as potential prey. Speak boldly and clearly, and bullies are likely to take their unwanted attention elsewhere.

Your voice is a great tool in portraying yourself as a self-assured person. A powerful, clear and confident tone radiates assertiveness and is great for deterring bullies.

It might not feel fair, but bullies make judgements about other kids very quickly. In a few seconds they can decide whether someone is a good target or whether they'd be better off bullying someone else. A confident speaking voice is a good tool for keeping bullies at bay. People who have been bullied regularly may be too quiet and their voice tone often lacks appropriate inflection. It may be monotone; sometimes it is loud, harsh, shrill or hostile.

You might be saying all the right things, but saying them in the wrong tone of voice can make you seem either too docile or argumentative. For example, if you whisper 'please leave me alone' in a timid voice, bullies are likely to ignore your message and continue to pick on you. Shouting isn't the answer, either. Losing your cool and using an angry voice can inflame bullies even more and keep them harassing you for an entertaining reaction.

Here's an idea for you...

Just like any other muscles, your vocal muscles need a regular work out to be on top form. Singing is a great way to exercise your voice. Singing for a few minutes every day can help you become more aware of your pitch and tone and you ought to notice improvements in your speaking voice. You don't need to be in the shower to sing, but some people find it helps.

Avoid being hesitant when you speak, preceding sentences with apologies, speaking quietly, allowing your sentences to trail off and using 'er' and 'um' a lot. All these things send a big message to bullies. They say 'I'm powerless'.

Instead:
- Aim to sound calm.
- Try not to mumble.
- Speak in a neutral, unemotional tone as if you were discussing what you had for lunch.
- Use a firm and steady voice, even if you feel shaky inside.
- Speak loudly without shouting.
- Always speak clearly.

While you are getting the hang of using your voice more assertively, even going part of the way towards your ultimate goals is fantastic. For example, if it is difficult to speak up, try using just one new technique from the list above. When you are proficient, try more techniques from the list, adding to your repertoire.

Many people raise their voice at the ends of sentences and this can also make them sound powerless. It's easy to counteract this by consciously dropping the tone of your voice at the end of sentences. It will make you sound more in control and self-assured, making it less likely that you will sound like a good target.

Tongue twisters are an enjoyable way to improve vocal agility; they give your jaw and facial muscles a good workout too. To practise sounding confident and assertive, record these ten tongue twisters every week and play them back to notice improvements:

■ A big bug bit the little beetle but the little beetle bit the big bug back.
■ If two witches were watching two watches, which witch would watch which watch?
■ Any noise annoys an oyster but a noisy noise annoys an oyster more.
■ A tutor who tooted the flute, tried to tutor two tooters to toot. Said the two to the tutor, 'Is it harder to toot or to tutor two tooters to toot?'
■ A proper copper coffee pot.
■ Around the rugged rocks the ragged rascals ran.
■ Vincent vowed vengeance very vehemently.
■ Fat frogs flying past fast.
■ She is a thistle sifter
   and she has a sieve of sifted thistles,
   and a sieve of unsifted thistles,
   and the sieve of unsifted thistles
   she sieves into the sieve of sifted thistles,
   because she is a thistle sifter.
■ These ten tricky tongue twisters trip thrillingly off the tongue.

Don't look at me in that tone of voice.
DAVID FARBER

Defining idea...

How did it go?

Q **My voice is breaking and people are picking on me because it sounds funny. How can I still sound assertive?**

A *The good news is that this voice breaking is temporary; it's the result of the hormone testosterone acting on your voice box. Testosterone is released into the body where it affects your vocal cords, making them longer and thicker. This makes them resonate less and results in a lower tone of voice. The great thing is that the breaking stage isn't going to last forever and that your voice is already on its way to sounding more manly and confident. I suggest you work on this idea anyway, so that when you have your new deep voice it will be filled with confidence.*

Q **I recently moved from Scotland to east London. Bullies are copying my accent. I hate it, what can I do?**

A *The best thing to do is to avoid showing the bullies how much this is bothering you. Having a confident, assertive tone of voice has nothing to do with your accent. As soon as they see that you are not intimidated, they will leave you alone. You can sound less intimidated whatever your accent, by practising and listening to the end of your sentences. When you make a statement, your voice should go down at the end of the sentence. If your intonation goes up at the end, you sound like you're asking a question or are unsure about what you said. Practice will help you become more confident.*

39

Because you're worth it

Bullying erodes self-esteem. But there is a lot that parents and teachers can do to increase kids' feelings of self-worth.

If anyone is constantly told that they're fat or stupid, they start to believe it. Self-esteem can be damaged by unkind comments, and by what bullies think and say.

Many children who are bullied are at risk of having problems with schoolwork, often find it hard to make friends, and are more likely to develop the mental-health problems like depression and anxiety that are related to low self-esteem.

Any one of the steps below will kick a child's self-esteem up a few notches. Do them all and you'll turbocharge it. Kids with high self-esteem will walk tall and sound more confident, both of which deter prospective bullies. A high sense of self-worth also immunises them against the toxic effects of bullying. Unkind words are less likely to linger or be believed. So here are some practical ways in which adults can help.

Notice when things are going well
As often as you can, catch your child being good. A simple word or touch to let your child know that you appreciate how good they are being will increase their self-esteem, so make sure that they know you've noticed what they've done.

Children who've been bullied often feel as if they are failures. When they make minor mistakes, they can beat themselves up over them excessively. If you've noticed this happening, let them know it's OK to make mistakes, and that everyone does. The most powerful way to do this is to talk about some mistakes you've made, and how you learned from them or put them right.

Focus on talents

Kids who have been bullied have had their weaknesses and shortcomings pointed out ad nauseam. They spend a lot of time in class unable to concentrate because they are preoccupied with bullies. Many miss school because they are afraid to go in and so fall behind, then feel overloaded with schoolwork and homework that they can't do because they weren't there in the first place. This is a recipe for feeling like a failure. Instead of focusing all resources on catching up on missed work, make sure there is dedicated time for them to develop their talents. If your son is rubbish at writing but has the makings of a champion surfer, make some time for him to get out on his surfboard and enter some competitions.

Split it up

You wouldn't expect a kid to eat a 1000g mega bar of chocolate in one sitting (although you could be surprised). You'd expect to break the chocolate up and share it in manageable pieces. When kids are overwhelmed, whether with dealing with bullies, homework or grappling to make friends, chunk each task into simple action steps so there's a sense of achievement at every one.

Let kids make decisions

Making simple decisions helps children feel powerful and in control. This is exactly the opposite of how being bullied makes people feel. Ask them questions that let them make decisions as often as you can. 'Shall we have pizza or fish tonight?' and 'which DVD would you like to watch after you've done your homework?' are good examples. Once they've chosen, respect their choice and don't make a fuss about it or try to redirect them towards your own preference.

You can calculate the worth of a man by the number of his enemies.
GUSTAVE FLAUBERT

Defining idea...

Stop nagging

Lots of parents don't even realise they are nagging or being critical. I suggest you spend a week really listening to yourself each time you speak to your children – and the chances are that you'll have a few unpleasant surprises. You are probably only trying to be helpful and improve things, but if you make a concentrated effort to use a gentle tone and upbeat words, encouraging rather than criticising, kids are more likely to flourish in all areas.

Put kids in charge

There are often areas where kids are responsible enough to be in charge. Start with something relatively simple, perhaps a cleaning or tidying chore, and then build up a greater number of responsibilities. As children develop competence in certain areas, and can complete simple tasks, diversify. Chores and tasks give kids a sense of accomplishment, achievement and maturity.

Exploit their expertise

Most children have expertise that they are not currently using at home. Many are more computer savvy than their parents, for example, and can be given responsibility for some things you do online, like grocery shopping. They're often much more au fait with technology in general, so perhaps they could be the ones to show granddad how to use his new mobile phone to send text messages? Being able to be an expert in an area like new technology helps bump up kids' self-esteem.

How did it go?

Q **My teenage daughter's self-esteem seems fine, even though she's been bullied. She's quite lippy and seems confident about expressing herself. How can I tell if it's just for show?**

A *It's tricky. Teenagers can be full of bravado, but on the other hand, she may well have a high sense of self-worth despite the bullying she's endured. Academic performance is a good barometer, so keep an eye on her schoolwork. A sudden drop in grades can be an indicator of low self-esteem.*

Q **My son's self-esteem is terrible. We've tried most of the things here, but it hasn't made much difference. Why not?**

A *Don't lose heart. It sounds as if you're making sterling efforts. It is perfectly possible to reverse the effect that bullying has on self-esteem, but this isn't a quick fix and can take many months. Keep going and you're likely to see some starry results from your endeavours.*

40

Home schooling

If bullying is so bad that your child is spending a lot of time at home, it might make sense to learn at home full time.

Some kids are so traumatised by bullying that they can't cope in classrooms. Home schooling may be a good solution.

I believe teaching children at home is a last resort. Before making this leap, it might be worth considering a change of school, which could sort out many problems. Unfortunately there are rare occasions when schools are unresponsive to a bullying problem or it just seems to take forever to sort out. When this happens, it is difficult for young people to access anything meaningful from a school curriculum, and many will be missing a lot of school because bullying has got out of hand. For this minority of children, home schooling may be a good idea.

Home schooling, which sometimes gets called home education, means that kids learn at home instead of at school. It's not a step to be taken lightly, and I'd encourage you to think through the pros and cons in some detail before making a final decision.

The pros are that children are removed from bullies, and family relationships are potentially closer. Home schooling can provide a more spontaneous and exciting education, with greater flexibility to pursue specific interests.

Here's an idea for you...

Why not speak to some home-schooling parents and young people to get their perspectives on what works and what doesn't? Your local education authority ought to be able to put you in touch with experienced home-schoolers. If there are none in your area, then there are many internet forums and people willing to share their ideas and expertise online. You know what they say – knowledge is power.

Now for the cons. Children are potentially with their family 24/7, all day, every day. There is usually some loss of income as one parent is normally the home educator and a reduction in family space in the house when this becomes a classroom or project area. The child also loses easy access to a peer group. In addition, it can be difficult for parents to be responsible for both education and parenting.

Many parents think that they will have to get special qualifications if they're interested in home schooling, but you don't have to be a teacher to teach your child at home. Rules vary from country to country, but in the UK children who are home schooled don't have to follow the National Curriculum or take national exams. The law obliges parents to make sure their children get full-time, age- and ability-appropriate education. You don't need anyone's permission to teach your child in your home, but you do have to let the school know in writing that you are removing your child from school and will be educating them at home. After that, it's pretty much over to you. You don't have to stick to conventional school days or term times. In other countries, rules are more complicated, and you may need to get special permission from education authorities.

There are a number of different educational philosophies that other home-schoolers have found useful, so let's look at them.

The Montessori Method

This educational approach developed out of the work of the Italian paediatrician Dr Maria Montessori in the early 1900s. Her aim was to scientifically study a child's true nature. Montessori home schools are buzzing with cultural, artistic and scientific activities. Children are encouraged to pursue their interests and are never forced to do set lessons or activities they don't want to take part in.

Traditional home schooling

Traditional home schooling is like school but at home, with lesson plans, a timetable, a classroom and subjects like maths, geography, etc. Many children follow the same curriculum that they would have done in school and many also sit national exams.

Unit studies

Home-schoolers following a unit-studies approach integrate a number of subjects into a topic or project. So, a project on the Egyptians could encompass history, geography, algebra, belly dancing and even making bead jewellery.

Eclectic

Adherents of the eclectic approach mix and match elements from different educational philosophies and do whatever works for their children.

Defining idea…

If you're going to keep your children out of schools you had better decide what an education means because no one is going to do it for you.
DAVID GUTERSON, author of *Family Matters: Why Homeschooling Makes Sense*

Defining idea…

We constantly questioned ourselves as parents – 'Are we doing the right thing? Are we ruining our child's life?' – as there really is no recipe for how to homeschool successfully. In the end we followed our gut feelings, we observed our only family and experience, and other homeschoolers, carefully and 'followed the child'.
JIM AND SUSAN STEPHENSON, experienced home educators

How did it go?

Q I've just started home schooling my son, and he seems happier away from the bullies and is learning better too. We both get a lot of questions when we are out in town during traditional school hours. People ask why he isn't at school, or if he has a day off. I know it's none of their business, but what can we say to get them off our backs?

A Say, 'He's taught at home and today he's learning how to deal with people who ask nosey questions'.

Q I'm concerned that my daughter will miss out on friends if we teach her at home. How can we make sure that doesn't happen?

A You're right to raise this. Children need to learn how to get on with others, and how to give and take. Lots of parents link up with other home-schoolers and often do some joint activities so kids don't need to miss out. You might also like to look at the range of sports and activity groups available locally. They give kids an opportunity to meet others away from school.

41
Seriously funny

Being bullied is no joke. But finding something to laugh at means you – and not the bully – can have the last laugh.

Learn to cope with bullying by focusing on any potential funnies. Humour is powerful and disarming to those who want to intimidate you.

I'd like to share a story about an eleven-year-old boy who used humour to ward off bullying. He's the son of a friend of mine, and when I heard his story, he said I could share it with some of the kids I see in clinic. I've changed his name, because he's quite a private boy, but the rest of the story is as he told it to me. Let's pretend he's called Eric. When he turned ten, Eric started in an after-school drama group. While the group was getting to know one another, they all wore sticky labels on which they wrote their names. At the first week, a bigger boy, Dillon, who wasn't as talented as Eric, started to pick on him, poking him and calling him an asshole. This happened the second week of drama too. On the third week, when everyone was writing their name labels, Eric wrote 'asshole' on his name label instead of his name, and wore it through the class. Everyone creased up, and the drama teacher realised what he was doing and didn't make a big deal of it. By making a joke of it, Eric removed Dillon's power, and took the hurt out of his insult. The other kids all laughed, and Eric became well liked. Dillon dropped out of drama a couple of weeks

Here's an idea for you...

This tip came from an internet bulletin board, and works well for playground bullies. In a public place and in the loudest voice you can muster, ask the bully, 'How long have you had Zachary Syndrome?' Then, when he or anyone else asks, 'What's that?' say to him in a very loud voice, so all the other kids can hear you, 'That's when your face looks ex-Zachary like your butt'. It's important not to laugh when you say this, as for maximum impact, you need to walk away while the onlookers are laughing. Doing that leaves the bully looking stupid and you looking confident. Result.

later. Not all humour tactics will have such a happy ending, but there is often a way to use humour to deflect a bully.

It's not a new idea. Way back at the turn of the twentieth century, Sigmund Freud thought that we human beings had developed a sense of humour as a way of defending ourselves or coping with hard times. Freud described a number of coping styles, which he called 'defence mechanisms'. He thought of these as automatic things that we do without thinking in order to protect ourselves against stress or danger. Humour, he believed, was a powerful defence mechanism.

So, what's Freud and his theory got to do with bullying? Quite a bit. Being able to laugh helps as it replaces upsetting feelings with enjoyable feelings. It also does something much more subtle. Introducing some humour into an exchange with bullies changes the meaning so that the bullies' words and actions are less powerful. Laughing has also often been shown to reduce stress as it gives us a different take on life. Searching for the funny side of even quite horrendous situations changes the way we think. You probably know this already, but feeling upset is closely linked to the way we think.

Several successful comedians have said that they learned to be funny at school to prevent people picking in them. The late, great Dudley Moore described himself as '… a very serious, pompous child. I spent the first seven years of my life siphoned off in hospital beds and wheelchairs with a club foot. It was my leg onto which I projected all my feelings of inadequacy and self-loathing'. At school he took to clowning to avoid the inevitable bullying and teasing.

One pay off from this could be that developing comic timing just might give you a career when you grow up!

We might be laughing a bit too loud, but that never hurt no one.
BILLY JOEL

Defining idea...

The bullying was hideous and relentless, and we turned it round by making ourselves celebrities.
JULIAN CLARY

Defining idea...

181

How did it go?

Q **Won't it provoke bullies if they are made fun of or ridiculed?**

A *Well, you're right that smiling or laughing can provoke bullies. When you turn a difficult situation into a funny one, the bully is caught off guard. Other children usually laugh and the bully ends up looking silly, not the victim. The trick in getting this to work is to make the situation funny, and to avoid laughing in front of the bully yourself. Let the others laugh instead.*

Q **There's a bigger girl who gets the same bus as me to school. She picks on me and I tell her I don't like it and she tells me I can stick it up my bum if I don't like it. It makes me cry. I want to try and make the other kids laugh so she will leave me alone. Can you give me some ideas?**

A *I feel for you having to be on that bus. There's a trick you can try that works for all those taunts to shove it or stick it. Why not say something like, 'I'd like to stick it up my bum, but my bum is full of all your other insults. Maybe in a day or two there'll be some room for new ones.' If you say it really loudly, other kids will hear and you should get a giggle.*

42

Call the cops

A stern word from the headteacher alone might not be enough if there's been an assault or other crime committed. Find out how and when to call the police.

It might not always feel that way, but schools are subject to the law. Assault, harassment and intimidation are crimes, whatever the age of the perpetrator or victim.

Making a complaint to the police about intimidation, physical attacks or threats is the best thing to do if the bullies are over the age of criminal responsibility. This varies in different countries but is ten years of age in England and Wales, for example. The police may be prepared to visit the bullies' homes to warn them off but it's unlikely that further action will follow unless there has been an assault with independent witnesses or a long campaign of harassment.

In some circumstances you should definitely call the emergency services, however:
- Where a serious injury has occurred.
- When a crime is in progress.
- If a suspect is on the scene.
- If a witness is likely to be lost if police do not attend imminently.
- If there is potential for carrying out a further crime.
- If a victim is severely distressed.

Here's an idea for you...

Knowledge is power. Instead of waiting for a serious bullying episode, why not approach your local police station and ask for written guidance on which types of bullying incidents they would respond to, and what a typical response might be? Armed with this information, you will be better placed to decide when and how to involve the police if something does happen, and what action to expect and request. Try to get hold of a named police contact, ideally a schools liaison officer, youth officer or hate-crime officer, and ask if you can circulate these details in the school. This sort of preventive action shows would-be bullies that you are serious and may therefore be a deterrent.

Perhaps the hardest decision about whether or not to involve the police is when things are not immediately urgent. These are the other times when it may possibly help to involve the police, but if it isn't an emergency, immediate police action often causes lots of trouble and angst. Parents and teachers may be hesitant about calling the police, or knowing when to do so. Schools act *in loco parentis* when kids are at school or involved in school-led activities, and so often resolve bullying incidents using their own disciplinary procedures.

Many areas now have a schools liaison officer or a youth liaison officer. I suggest involving them when a bullying incident could have serious consequences for a victim. The problem is that making this judgement can prove next to impossible as almost any bullying can have potentially serious long-term consequences for the person on the receiving end. Be guided by the victim, and if in doubt, consult with the police and take their advice. Bear in mind that many of the actions we call bullying are also crimes. For example, hitting or kicking is an assault and extortion is a kind of theft.

Everyone has the right to report to the police any incident which they consider may be illegal. I'd also suggest involving police when other anti-bullying approaches have failed and it seems likely that reporting it will make the bullying less likely to recur. Involving the police sends a powerful message that bullying is unacceptable.

If you do report bullying to the police, be ready to tell them several things:

- Exactly what happened.
- When and how often it has happened.
- Where the incident(s) took place.
- Who was involved.
- Who else saw it happen.
- What action you have taken, if any.

It's worth keeping in mind that teachers, parents and young people are often able to resolve incidents more quickly themselves than if the police are involved. Even if an incident does go to court, there's no guarantee of a successful outcome.

All students and their families have the right to feel safe and secure within the school environment.
DETECTIVE SERGEANT BRENDAN MEARS, of Lower Hutt, New Zealand

Defining idea…

Police arrested two kids yesterday. One was drinking battery acid, the other was eating fireworks. They charged one and let the other off.
TOMMY COOPER

Defining idea…

How did it go?

Q **What can I do if my child is being bullied by children below the age of criminal responsibility?**

A *If there has been serious violence or if the bullying has been protracted, I think it is worth seeking police advice in any case. There may be little they can do but, on the other hand, police can refer troubled children – including bullies – to professional agencies, and this may be indirectly helpful to you.*

Q **My son was beaten up by bullies in school and left with bruises. I was shocked to find the school didn't report it to the police as he was quite badly hurt. They told me they didn't think that it would help to sort things out. How can I get them to change their mind?**

A *I'm sorry to hear about your son. It's important to appreciate that even if a school does not report an incident, this does not prevent anyone else from doing so. You might also opt to have these bruises and injuries recorded by a medical practitioner. If you do decide to make a report, the police will decide whether further action is suitable. They might talk to the children involved or agree on a proper response with teachers. If the police think there is good evidence that a significant incident has occurred, they may be able to charge someone.*

43

Making a drama out of a crisis

Putting on a play about bullying can build kids' self-confidence, empathy and assertive communication skills. Here's a great way to have fun and beat the bullies at the same time.

Not many bully-busting activities are stimulating, energised, entertaining and educational. But creating and staging a powerful drama about bullying can be all of those things.

For a powerful and memorable way to deal with bullies, while also learning more about their motivation and our responses, nothing beats drama. Drama teaches interpretation, personal creativity and new ways of looking at the same information. For millennia, human beings have used drama to communicate powerful emotions, from Greek tragedies to Italian *commedia dell'arte* to Balinese shadow puppet theatre and French farce. Just think about the variety of films around, too. Whatever genre you plump for, there are different approaches to use with a group of kids, which work slightly differently. Have a go at these.

Here's an idea for you...

If you know that a particular child or specific group of children has been bullied, then suggest that they write, cast, rehearse and perform a play about it. Writing about their experience and performing their drama with a cast of friendly goodies and baddies can help both them and others – not necessarily those directly involved, either – understand bullying from different perspectives. It also gives them a way to ensure that they have a happy ending on stage even if there wasn't such a neat one in real life. Rehearsing and performing different ways of dealing with the bullies can help those with first-hand experience learn how to do it off-stage, too.

Group role play

In group role play, a group of children or young people select a bullying theme from the following list and improvise a short play around it:

- Name calling;
- Stealing someone's stuff;
- Teasing;
- Shunning;
- Racist bullying;
- Intimidation;
- Bus-stop bullying;
- Bullying on the way to school;
- Cyber bullying.

Being able to improvise creative solutions to these common bullying scenarios is an effective way of resolving potential conflicts. It helps kids value those who are different or who hold different views. It is also important for agreeing common values, problem solving, developing social skills, rehearsing action plans and improving the overall awareness of bullying.

Each group might be given the same topic, but will probably choose to work on different areas; they might focus on problem solving, developing understanding, making decisions or empathising with others through playing different roles, for instance. Role reversal, where kids use a variety of roles, helps build empathy skills. For example, an actual or potential bully in the group will have an opportunity to play a victim and understand what that feels like during role reversal, and the usual victims – or possible victims, of course – would play the bullies. Through role play kids are also able to observe their own actions and make observations about themselves in a safe setting which is also fun.

Writing new drama

Once the group is comfortable with spontaneous improvisations, they will be ready to write some of their own drama. Encourage all the children to write, rehearse and present short dramatic sketches or plays developing the bullying scenarios that they started during improvisation.

We need a type of theatre which not only releases the feelings, insights and impulses possible within the particular historical field of human relations in which the action takes place, but employs and encourages those thoughts and feelings which help transform the field itself.
BERTOLT BRECHT

Defining idea...

Staging an existing play about bullying

There is abundant convincing evidence from research that young people exposed to theatre arts training perform better in school, have more consistent attendance, demonstrate more empathetic behaviour towards others and have greater self-esteem. Learning and putting on a play about bullying activates vivacity and stimulates kids physically, emotionally, socially and intellectually. There are many plays about bullying to choose from, so check some of them out. These are my favourites:

- *The Secret Life of Girls* by Linda Doughtery
- *I Met a Bully on the Hill* by Maureen Hunter and Martha Brooks
- *The Bully Show!* by Brian Guehring
- *Apparently Not* by Hayley Gordon
- *The Bully* by Jan Needle
- *Nutter, an Anti-Bullying Play for Young People* by the London Bus Theatre Company
- *The Mirror of Tears* by Libby Hughes

Whichever of these three types of dramatic intervention you opt for, it's worth remembering that drama is a powerful technique. End each session with a brief discussion about bullying and how it can be stopped and prevented.

How did it go?

Q **We're putting on an anti-bullying play that students have written themselves. There will be younger brothers and sisters in the audience and I've been looking for ideas about how we can support them if anything presented on stage resonates with their own experience. Have you got some I can use?**

A *Feelings often run high, including during rehearsals and post-performance. Strong emotions can linger long after the final curtain call. It's worth thinking of ways in which all the children can discuss these feelings. You could consider giving out a national bullying helpline number or printing it on the programme, and even having a box where kids in the audience can post their experiences of being bullied too.*

Q **I'm keen to help kids develop assertive body language through drama techniques. Their verbal abilities have improved, but they still don't all look as confident as they could and some are definitely nervous. Any suggestions?**

A *I suggest you go back to some improvisation work, but encourage the kids to keep their improvisations to six lines as an absolute maximum. They will then need to be more reliant on body language to convey messages, and more assertive body language will gradually develop as they develop the skills to make themselves understood using gesture and stance rather than dialogue.*

44

You've been framed

A great way to fight back against bullying is to shoot. As in film.

Making an anti-bullying video — and sharing it with others — is a wonderful way to unleash your creativity. May your on-screen action speak louder than the bullies' words!

Some particularly sinister bullies film their heinous crimes on phones and share them with other thugs. But you don't have to be a bully to know that films are fun to make; you can get in on the action with an anti-bullying film. As they say on YouTube, broadcast yourself. Movie making is empowering too, and you may even make some new friends while you are doing it.

Luke Hupton from Manchester in the UK made a hard-hitting feature length film about a girl who was bullied so severely that she committed suicide. He is studying film direction and made the film aged just eighteen. He says he drew largely on his own experiences of being victimised and bullied at school. He explained: 'It is about something that is important to me and I wrote the first draft of the script in the summer that I left school.'

Here's an idea for you...

What are you waiting for? Unleash your creativity on the small screen. Beg or borrow a mobile phone with a camera and start recording your own anti-bullying film. Don't worry too much about camera shake and angles. The main thing is to get going. And remember what artists say, having no money means you have no restrictions.

Making an anti-bullying film might sound complicated, but it can be really straightforward. You don't have to have any formal training in order to make a simple film you can share online. In the recent past, if you wanted to make a film and exploit the advantages of this direct form of communication, you had to invest in equipment that was way beyond the budget of most schoolchildren, but now making a film and sharing it is within almost everyone's reach. Get a mobile phone with a video camera. Get shooting. Easy peasy. And you can do it on the cheap too. Remember that stories told through film are easier for people to relate to, as they can see and hear what is happening.

First off, you need to think about whether you are going to be the subject of your film or the camera operator, or both. Once you've decided, think about where you want to set it. You might want to make a video diary of an anti-bullying day, for instance opening with kids standing up to bullies on the school bus, or of a group of friends being kind to people. If you are making the film with others, it is worth planning a few rehearsal sessions first.

Lights
Get your lighting right, and the rest of your film stands high chances of having some professional flair and polish. Think about lighting yourself while you are speaking into the camera. Again, don't worry about fancy equipment, just pack a torch.

Camera

You really don't need an amazing, high-end camcorder or Hollywood editing suite to make a decent movie. With half of all phones now having video capacity, there is probably some film-making equipment within borrowable reach. Granted, you're not going to get camcorder quality from mobile phones, but as long as you can get hold of one with a largish pixel count and heaps of storage, you'll be fine.

I really approached the film as if it was a white big piece of paper and I was just going to draw a picture on it. And whether that picture was good or bad, whatever people thought of it, what they could never take away was that it was my picture.
BENJAMIN DISRAELI

Defining idea...

Action

All the action should be in the shot, not in your hand as you hold the camera. Keep things simple for your first few films by keeping just one or two people in each shot. Having lots of people and swinging the camera between them will make your audience feel sick. Audience? More later. Your aim is to capture memorable actions, not hours of people talking worthily. While the action is happening, think about different viewpoints. Could you crouch down low and film upwards, or climb up on a table and film down?

Share

It's good to share. When you've made your anti-bullying film, transfer it onto your hard drive, edit it and then upload it onto a movie-sharing site like YouTube.

The length of a film should be directly related to the length of a human bladder.
ALFRED HITCHCOCK

Defining idea...

How did
it go?

Q **What do you think about using film to try to catch bullies and prove what they have done?**

A *That's an important question. This is really all about making a positive, upbeat film to counteract bullying. You're asking about filming bullying activity. If you witness bullying, it's unusual for the safest action for you to be filming it. It is usually much better to either get a parent or teacher or, in an emergency, to call the police. Filming bullying might perversely encourage the bullies, who could feel that you were giving them an audience. There's also the matter of what you do with the film. If you film people without their permission, you're on shaky ground. If you happen to catch some bullying action while making a film, that's a different matter and you should share this film with an adult or with the police.*

Q **How can making a film and uploading it do much against bullying?**

A *It's about visibly taking a stand. Many celebrities have recorded anti-bullying messages and uploaded them. Being courageous and adding your voice and your positive message adds weight to the growing anti-bullying community. Watching films helps us discover our common humanity.*

45

Making a bully a friend

This idea isn't for the faint-hearted and it doesn't work for all bullies, but if you can make a bully a friend, you lose a bully and gain a mate.

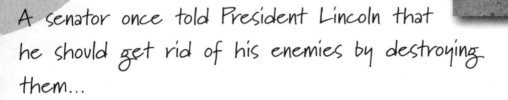

A senator once told President Lincoln that he should get rid of his enemies by destroying them...

Lincoln said, I agree with you sir, and the best way to destroy an enemy is to make him a friend. Now, although you probably sometimes feel like giving bullies a taste of their own medicine, bullying back is never the answer. Being friendly might be the last thing on your mind, but it could just work.

Some kids bully because they are mean and nasty. Other kids bully because they are hurt, angry, feeling left out or lonely. Befriending the ones like this means you are less likely to be bullied by them and can even help them to stop bullying. However, there are some people it isn't advisable to be friends with. If the bullies are in trouble all the time, into drugs or shoplifting, then it is worth giving them a miss on your next party invitation list. Most bullies have a group of hangers-on, who often do some bullying but are not as bad as the ringleaders. These hangers-on are often potential mates.

Another word of warning. The more manipulative bullies may turn on you later or try to get you involved in bullying. If you do successfully befriend a bully, make sure

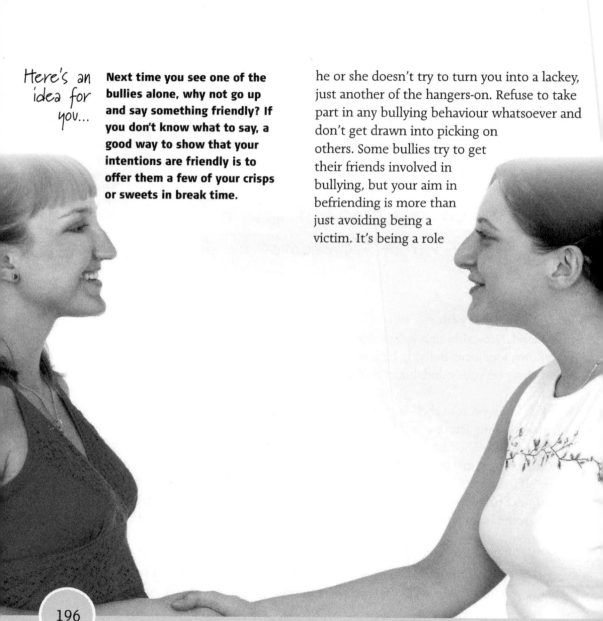

Here's an idea for you...

Next time you see one of the bullies alone, why not go up and say something friendly? If you don't know what to say, a good way to show that your intentions are friendly is to offer them a few of your crisps or sweets in break time.

he or she doesn't try to turn you into a lackey, just another of the hangers-on. Refuse to take part in any bullying behaviour whatsoever and don't get drawn into picking on others. Some bullies try to get their friends involved in bullying, but your aim in befriending is more than just avoiding being a victim. It's being a role model of what a good friend is, too. Once you have made friends with a bully, you might be able to share what it felt like to be picked on and how good it feels to be friends instead. So let's look at how you might do this.

Darkness cannot drive out darkness; only light can do that. Hate cannot drive out hate; only love can do that.
MARTIN LUTHER KING

Defining idea…

Being kind to bullies often confuses them. If a bully comes up to you and says, 'Shove off, that's my seat', you smiling and replying, 'Would you like to sit next to me?' is likely to stop the bully in his or her tracks. Some children bully others verbally because they feel intimidated. Being friendly and letting them get to know you as a person, rather than just someone they pick on, often dispels their sense of intimidation and diminishes their enthusiasm for bullying. Bullies might look surprised or react weirdly when you first do this. They're often not good at making friends, so might not know how to respond. Rather than emphasising and dwelling on bullying behaviour, focusing on being friendly is frequently much more productive and powerful.

As the Buddhist teaching says, stability in life is an illusion; life is constantly changing and we are always changing. This means bullies can change too. Some changes are more noticeable and apparent than others. It means that the more we look for small changes, the more we will notice the changes. Therefore, noticing and paying attention to small changes can set in motion more and more changes and since we are all

Now, it's very obvious to you that your bullies are treating you like an enemy. What you don't realise is that you are treating them like an enemy, too.
IZZY KALMAN, psychologist and author of *Bullies to Buddies*

Defining idea…

changing, the focus is on how to direct our attention to more positive changes that are already going on. Bullies might not become saints overnight, but there are likely to be little changes in their behaviour that become progressively more friendly.

How did it go?

Q **It seems a bit fake to be friendly to a bully, but I have noticed I get an easier time when I am polite to the bullies. They definitely leave me be. I don't like being phoney, though. What do you think?**

A *It sounds as if the idea is working. You don't have to become best buddies and sometimes being friendly is enough. It probably does feel fake to be nice to the bullies, but if a few smiles and polite words get them off your back, I reckon it's a small price to pay.*

Q **I have tried being friendly to the bullies, but now my best mate says she won't hang round with me any more if I am nice to them. What can I do?**

A *It sounds as if she might feel a bit left out or confused about you being nice to the bullies. If you haven't already done this, why not explain to her why you are trying to do this? See if you can persuade her to join you in a best mates anti-bullying effort. It isn't fair of her to make her friendship conditional on who else you are nice to. Why not say something like, 'I will always think of you as my best mate, and if you don't want to be my mate because I'm trying this new way to stop bullying, I'd be really sad, but it's your choice'. Once she realises it's her decision, she's very unlikely to forgo your friendship.*

46

Anti-bullying week

Use the designated international anti-bullying weeks to create bold new initiatives in schools and community groups.

Spending an out-and-out week to focus attention on bullying and ways to combat it is a great way to change the outlook of a whole school or youth group.

Many people will remember that on 20 April 1999, the US's worst school shooting took place at Columbine High School in Littleton, Colorado. Thirteen students and a teacher were killed, and twenty-three other students were wounded. The two young attackers, who had been bullied by their schoolmates, also died. In the aftermath, teachers, school pupils and parents across the US were determined to do something positive and educational in memory of this tragedy.

In remembrance of the Columbine shootings, and as a symbol of the year-round struggle against bullying, the third week in April is now a designated anti-bullying week. Canada has its own national bullying awareness week, later in the year. In the UK, anti-bullying awareness week usually takes place in autumn.

Here's an idea for you...

Why not make a short anti-bullying video in your school during the awareness week? You could post it on YouTube, as part of an innovative anti-bullying resource for other young people. Celebrities including Leona Lewis, Girls Aloud, Dannii Minogue and Arsene Wenger have posted personal video messages on the Beatbullying channel on YouTube. Upload your own anti-bullying videos and messages and be part of the world's biggest anti-bullying drive.

There are several reasons for having an anti-bullying week. It raises awareness of bullying and acknowledges that bullying is serious and destructive. It also identifies the fact that bullying is unacceptable, and helps everyone be aware of the reasons people bully and the different types of bullying. Finally, it's a good way to celebrate successful anti-bullying initiatives, and it needn't be confined to schools.

Before anti-bullying week, take some time to discover what children, young people and parents want in and from their schools. Consider having some of these hopes printed on postcards and distribute them around the school. Hold a meeting to see how best these wishes could be addressed, and which initiatives could be launched in the week. It takes more than a week to address bullying, but if you can persuade your school, church, youth group or even young ornithologists group to sign up for a couple of the following activities, you're off to a brilliant start.

Take your pick from these suggested activities.
- Hold a special assembly each day covering a different theme, for example:
  Monday: bullying in the playground
  Tuesday: cyber bullying
  Wednesday: homophobic bullying
  Thursday: racist and religious bullying

Friday: an award ceremony to recognise those pupils and teachers who have made a special contribution against bullying.

- Invite a speaker from an anti-bullying charity or organisation to make an evening presentation about an aspect of bullying that parents may be less familiar with from their schooldays, focusing on what they can do as parents and giving them opportunities to try out the technology in the case of something like cyber bullying.
- Kids could make a special effort to speak to someone who doesn't have anyone to talk to in the playground.
- Make a short film about bullying.
- Put on a play that draws attention to bullying.
- Set up an anti-bullying poster competition.
- Compose a peaceful piece of music or an angry anti-bullying rap.
- Schools could use the week to launch a new initiative like a school bus parent volunteer rota or a bully court.
- Start a graffiti wall where people can spray or paint ideas to combat bullying and anti-bullying statements.
- Ask every child to think of one idea to tackle bullying, which they write down on a piece of paper. You then collate all the answers, taking out similar ones, write them up into a document and present to the kids.
- Write anti-bullying letters and send them to MPs.
- Schools could also use the week to review the school anti-bullying policy with all stakeholders.

Defining idea...

More than half of young people in schools are being bullied, and one in ten are bullied severely. In order to reduce the number of incidents, school communities need a range of responses involving young people participating in the development of anti-bullying strategies.
ALISON O'BRIEN, NSPCC Education Adviser

How did it go?

Q **A few years ago I noticed that kids and teachers were wearing blue wristbands for bullying awareness week. What's happened to them?**

A *They're still around, and some people are still wearing blue wristbands to show their stance against bullying. However, there was a dreadful backlash in some areas where bullies started to calculatingly target kids who were wearing the wristbands, so they are not as widespread as they once were. In light of this, they are perhaps not the most effective way of raising awareness of bullying. It is sad when an initiative like this increases bullying, and blue wristbands may be best avoided.*

Q **How can we keep the ideas and momentum generated in anti-bullying awareness week going through the year?**

A *Anti-bullying initiatives work best when they are an embedded part of school and social curricula. Few survive without thoughtful and continual attention. Try not to think of anti-bullying week in isolation, but view the activities as either a launch pad for continuing initiatives or a forum for generating ideas that will continue through the year. You might like to consider holding meetings to review anti-bullying activities to make sure they don't get lost as the school year progresses. It can be hard to take time to focus on future issues or to reflect on past progress when current activities demand immediate attention. Many schools schedule special meetings two or three times a year that are devoted to assessing their anti-bullying initiatives' progress, focus and direction.*

47

Goal

Some kids seem to succeed at coping with bullying, while others struggle. Give your efforts an extra boost by focusing on goal setting.

Goal-directed bully busting is the way to go. Do you know the old adage, unless you know where you're headed, you won't know how to get there?

Way back in the 1950s, a group of researchers at Yale University looked at goal setting in some detail. They asked graduates about their goal-setting habits and followed their progress over twenty years. They found that the 3% of graduates with clearly written goals in the 1950s were worth more money than the other 97% put together. They were also healthier and had more stable relationships.

What's this got to do with bullying? Well, set yourself achievable targets on the basis of what you can realistically achieve, and work step by step to develop your potential and immunise yourself against effects of bullying. Try thinking for a moment of anti-bullying goals as targets you want to achieve. By goals I mean something quite unlike hopes or wishes which are not usually linked to an action plan. When you set bully-busting goals, and write them down, you are much more likely to succeed.

Here's an idea for you...

If it's hard to write down goals, why not draw a picture of what successful bully busting would look like? What would you be doing? Where would you be doing it? Who else would be there? How would onlookers know you are successful at beating the bullies? Once you have this image on paper, it will be easier to set goals.

There are other ways you can give your goals some extra kick. First off, express them positively. 'Put a complaint about this bullying in writing to the headteacher' is a more powerful goal than something like 'don't let the bullies get to you'. Goals are more effective if you make a deal with yourself that you will actually do them. How? By setting a SMART goal (more below), putting in dates, times and amounts so that your success can be measured.

Now, you may already have a number of coping goals. They might be like these: to get through a school day without being bullied, making some friends who are kind and will look out for you, feeling able to concentrate on homework instead of thinking about bullying. When you have a number of goals, the way to make them happen is to give each a priority. If you don't, the chances are that you'll start feeling overwhelmed by all the things you have to do.

You already know that goals are more powerful when written down, and some people like to keep a diary of goals for the month or week. However you decide to do this, it's really important to keep your goals small and do-able. When goals are too big, it often feels as if you are not progressing.

Great goals
Another way to boost your goals is to keep them SMART. Here's how:

Specific. When a goal is specific, it's easier to know when it's been achieved. Aim to write your goal as a detailed description of what you want to see happen. For example, 'I will be able to travel on the school bus without feeling threatened or intimidated or having any of my property taken', is a more specific goal than 'I want to get rid of the bullying problem'.

Measurable. If your goals are measurable, you will know when you have achieved them. You can make anti-bullying goals measurable in terms of frequency of bullying incidents, the intensity of their effect on you and the number of bully-free days or the number of times you have tried a particular idea.

Action based. Bully busters have to know exactly what they need to do. You will need to have a set of actions that will help you achieve your goal. For example, 'I will decrease the chances the bus bullies will pick on me by sitting close to the driver on no fewer than six out of ten bus journeys each week'.

Realistic. Goals have to be within reach. I don't mean that you should set goals for things you can do already, but that you should aim to pitch them slightly outside of your comfort zone, but not in the 'that-would-really-freak-me-out zone'.

Time bound. Setting time scales for each of your goals is important. Try to make a time each week to build in regular reviews of your progress.

What are you waiting for? Grab a pen and some paper and write down some anti- bullying goals for the next month, using the SMART technique.

I can't change the direction of the wind, but I can adjust my sails to always reach my destination.
JIMMY DEAN, singer

Defining idea...

It's not the mountain we conquer, but ourselves.
EDMUND HILLARY

Defining idea...

Celebrate victories

There's no point achieving all these victories if they go unnoticed. The drawback of many small steps is that you often don't have a moment where it all feels like a huge attainment. You have to create those moments by celebrating success. If you have successfully spoken back to a bully, or walked off and ignored hurtful comments, these are triumphs and ought to be celebrated as such.

How did it go?

Q I've set myself some ambitious anti-bullying goals but I think they're a bit heavy and now I feel like giving up. What do you suggest?

A *Setting goals at the right level takes practice, so don't be too ambitious. Have another go. Try to set goals that are out of your immediate reach, that stretch you, but not so hard that they are unattainable. With practice you will become skilled at setting goals that you have more than an 80% chance of achieving.*

Q I find it really hard to know if I've achieved a goal. How can I be sure?

A *Ask yourself before starting on a new goal how you would know if you were successful. Write it down and look at it often. When you get there, it's time to celebrate.*

48

Professional help

Bullying affects mental health; kids who are bullied are more likely to become depressed, anxious and have suicidal thoughts. You may feel your child needs help. Here's how.

Lots of people claim they'll help children who have been bullied. But what do all those letters mean and what can these guys do for you?

A study carried out at King's College, London, shows that children who are bullied are more likely to develop depression and anxiety. Dr Louise Arsenault and her team studied 1116 pairs of twins born between 1994 and 1995. Among identical twin pairs where one twin was bullied and the other was not, the bullied twin was much more likely to have psychological problems including depression and anxiety.

But where do you turn if problems like these are affecting your child? Qualifications can be confusing. How can you know if something like 'CRCP' means your doctor has a certificate from the regional college of psychiatrists or just an advanced interest in potholing? Unsurprisingly, there are different recognised qualifications for people doing different jobs, and they vary, so let's look at them – and at what these people can do for your child.

Psychiatrists

There's a lot of rubbish written about psychiatrists. Many people think patients will be made to lie on a couch, interpret ink blots and talk about their mother. This is

Here's an idea for you...

Talking about money can be difficult. The first thing you may need to establish is whether the treatment is available in the public sector, or if you will have to pay for it. If you're paying, it's vital to ask how much you will be charged per session. You could also try asking if the person who will be treating your child charges differently according to parental income – that's called a sliding scale.

not the case at all. A psychiatrist is a doctor, with a degree in medicine and postgraduate training in detecting, diagnosing and treating mental, emotional and behavioural disorders. They're also able to prescribe medication. Letters to look for:

- MBBS (medical degree)
- MD (medical degree in some countries; confusingly it's a postgraduate research degree in others)
- MRCPsych, FRCPsych (member or fellow of the Royal College of Psychiatrists)
- MMed Psych, FF Psych, FC Psych (alternatives to MRCPsych in some countries)
- FRANZCP (Fellow of the Royal Australian and New Zealand College of Psychiatrists)

Psychiatric nurses

These are all-round great guys. They're qualified nurses with specialist training, skills and knowledge in treating a range of mental, emotional and behavioural disorders. As well as administering medication, many nurses are trained in one or more talking treatments. In this case look for the letters RMN (registered mental nurse).

Psychotherapists

Psychotherapists use talking to assuage depression, explore feelings and relationships. Those who work with children usually use weekly play sessions, meeting at the same time and place, and lasting for fifty minutes. Bona fide psychotherapists are members of overseeing bodies like the United Kingdom Council for Psychotherapy (UKCP) and the British Association of Counselling and

Psychotherapy (BACP), but unfortunately anyone can call themselves a psychotherapist. Do check up.

Clinical psychologists

Clinical psychologists have an honours degree in psychology and have done further postgraduate study. Their job usually involves testing and therapy based on the belief that damaging behaviours can be unlearned and changing unhelpful thoughts, but they can't prescribe drugs. Look for the letters BSc and PhD, here.

The first meeting should be an assessment. Firstly, prepare your child for her first session by making a list of symptoms; this can be invaluable and helps the person you are seeing plan treatment. At the end of your assessment, get answers to these questions:

- Is there a formal diagnosis or name for the problems she's experiencing?
- How many times do you think she'll need to see you?
- How long will her appointments be?
- What type of treatment do you offer and is it proven in any way?
- How long does this treatment take?
- Are we able to contact you between appointments and how can we get in touch? (For example, a behavioural psychologist may encourage email feedback; some psychotherapists discourage phone contact between sessions.)

Psychiatrist: a man who asks you a lot of expensive questions that your wife asks you for nothing.
SAM BARDELL

Defining idea...

He is always saying he is some sort of nerve specialist because it sounds better but everyone knows he is just some sort of janitor in a looney bin.
P. G. WODEHOUSE

Defining idea...

How did it go?

Q **My daughter's had loads of problems with bullying and seems depressed and preoccupied. Her teacher has referred her to a school guidance counsellor. What's the difference between a counsellor and a psychotherapist?**

A *Counselling helps with specific problems or a crisis. Person-centred counselling is an opportunity to talk about how you feel about yourself, other people in your life and things that have affected you. Psychotherapists tend to focus on childhood experiences, dreams, your unconscious mind and the dynamics of your relationship with them. But, there's no unambiguous difference and the names are used interchangeably. As a general rule, counsellors employed in schools or voluntary agencies help people manage everyday problems, like bullying and exam stress, rather than the severe mental illness that is often referred to psychotherapists, but there are many exceptions.*

Q **The actual bullying seems much better but I'd like my son to see a psychiatrist as I think he might be depressed. I don't know how to arrange this. There are so many in the phone book and I can't decide between them. What's the best way?**

A *It's different in different countries. In some countries, including the UK, your GP should be your first port of call as they act as gatekeepers to medical specialists. In other countries, like Germany, you can contact a psychiatrist directly. You could also phone community child and adolescent mental health clinics and ask how to get referred.*

213

49

It's a dog's life

Animals are great antidotes to bullying. It's hard to feel stressed or grumpy when there's a cat or dog snuggling up, offering unconditional affection.

A four-legged friend like a dog or cat can help bullied children rediscover how to relate to others and feel loved, and restore their sense of self-worth.

We're used to seeing dogs leading the blind or assisting the deaf, but did you know pets can help nurse you back to health when you're feeling low? Pets can offer valuable support and stress relief when bullying takes its toll. This is no shaggy dog story; they really can make a difference.

Firstly, pets bring fun to dull days, introduce your child to new friends and never tire of their owner's voice. They won't ditch their owners, either, when times are tough and nobody seems to care. Instead they offer friendship and pleasure that can help ward off the sadness and isolation that can come from bullying. Hildegard George, a psychotherapist, has said that animals can teach children how to relax and be themselves. She believes that animals are often better for children than toys because animals constantly bring the child back to the reality of the relationship.

Here's an idea for you...

Actually owning a pet may be impractical, but don't let that stop you involving animals in your child's life. If having something like a dog at home is impossible, they might enjoy helping out at the local animal shelter.

The Chimo project in Alberta, Canada is at the forefront of pet therapy. Here therapists are trained to use dogs, cats, rabbits and other animals to help people with all sorts of difficulties, including children who have been bullied. A psychologist working at the Chimo project used a cat to help a boy who was in this situation. The boy thought of this cat as a safe friend – especially as the cat, who had previously been in an animal shelter, had been bullied by the other cats at the shelter. The child felt that the cat understood him, and consequently liked the cat very much. He remarked that he felt safe with the cat because she wouldn't say, 'Shut up, you fatso', which was how the children at school had taunted him. While the boy talked about his problems, he petted the cat, snuggled with her and focused on the cat instead of on his therapist.

Professor Odendaal, a South African researcher, studied six people with depression who all had a daily visit from a dog that lasted half an hour. Before the study, all six had low blood levels of chemicals responsible for creating feelings of enjoyment and happiness. After meeting the dogs, the levels of these key chemicals increased in their blood stream. More importantly, they felt happier too. Remember that depression is a common and significant health risk associated with bullying, as is stress, and you can see that the benefits of pet ownership may help your bullied child. Here are some others which can also help repair damaged self-esteem and combat the effects of stress.

- It doesn't matter if it's a lizard or a llama – pets stop you feeling lonely.
- Caring for a four-legged friend gives a child's life meaning and mitigates against the painful effects of being bullied.
- Pets need their owners. They offer them a sense of being wanted when you feel the world's against them.
- Walking the dog widens most people's circle of friends.
- Animals get kids out, whereas being bullied can make them feel like curling up indoors.
- Pets offer companionship and non-judgemental affection.
- Stroking furry animals relieves stress by lowering both blood pressure and pulse rate.
- Pets give a child something to nurture and care for. Kids who have a pet to look after have a higher sense of self-worth.

However, you do need to consider that owning a pet is a big commitment and responsibility; it's not a decision to be taken lightly. Yes, animals offer warmth and company, but many have heavy-duty needs of their own. Involve children in the choice of pet, advising and guiding their decision, and make it clear that you expect them to be equally involved in looking after their new friend.

Instinctively, we know pets make us feel good. Scientifically, we can trace those 'feel good' emotions to chemical reactions in people that are triggered by pets.
DR REBECCA JOHNSON, professor of Gerontological Nursing and Public Policy

Defining idea...

How did it go?

Q **My teenage son has been depressed after relentless bullying. As he now finds it quite hard to trust people and make new friends, his father and I have been thinking about getting him a puppy. He likes animals and is a responsible lad, but we don't want it to become a burden and stress him out with extra responsibility. What's your advice?**

A *Pets have helped people of all ages get over depression. Your son needs to be well enough for the intensive work necessary when looking after a puppy, otherwise your worries about overburdening him might turn out to be true. Have you thought about getting an older dog from a rescue home? Nurturing a special friend like this may give him the boost he needs, without the extra burdens that come with puppies. Before you rush out to the pet shop or dogs' home, speaking to your son about what he'd find most helpful will go a long way towards ensuring you make the right decision.*

Q **My daughter's been bullied and likes the idea of getting a dog to protect her and scare the bullies off. What do you think?**

A *I think absolutely not, but I can see why she's considered it. Pet dogs are great companions, but mustn't be thought of as a potential weapon or trained in such a way. There are some dogs that are used as guard dogs, but they are not pets, and they don't give people all the benefits linked to pet ownership.*

50

Remember to breathe

When the pressure of being bullied bites hard, these easy breathing techniques are just what the doctor ordered.

Consider this an invitation to reduce the tension that invariably comes with bullying. Breathing awareness reduces stress, is portable and free. Give it a go.

Childhood ought to be carefree and relaxing, but bullying frequently makes it the opposite. The damage inflicted by bullying is commonly underestimated. Dr Stephen Joseph, a psychologist at Warwick University, led a research project which studied 331 pupils in England. His team found 40% had been bullied at some time. About a third of those bullied children showed signs of stress, including:

- Feeling bad about themselves.
- Finding it hard to get to sleep.
- Having nightmares.
- Experiencing explosive rages.
- Having headaches.
- Showing increased jumpiness.
- Avoiding the place where the bullying took place.
- Having tummy aches.
- Feeling sick.

Here's an idea for you...

This breath-counting exercise has been devised by Dr Weil, a leading integrative medicine practitioner. Sit in a comfortable position with your spine straight and head inclined slightly forward. Gently close your eyes and take a few deep breaths. Then let the breath come naturally without trying to influence it. Ideally it will be quiet and slow, but depth and rhythm may vary. To begin the exercise, count 'one' to yourself as you exhale. The next time you exhale, count 'two', and so on up to 'five'. Then begin a new cycle, counting 'one' on the next exhalation. Never count higher than 'five' and count only when you exhale. You will know your attention has wandered when you find yourself up to 'eight', 'twelve' or even 'nineteen'. Try to do this for ten minutes.

- Having lots of worries.
- Being tearful.
- Being hypersensitive.
- Having poor concentration.

If any of these seem at all familiar, it's possible that you are suffering from bully-related stress. Breathing awareness can help children and young people reduce stress and also promotes feelings of relaxation. No, you don't have to chant 'om', eat lentils or assume the lotus position (but it's cool if you want to). Once you have learned this technique, you can do it anywhere, at any time. At the risk of sounding like a prissy trombone teacher, for great results it's best to practise every day.

The brain automatically controls breathing, including breath size and frequency, based on signals from sensors in the lungs. When stress levels rise, the rate at which our lungs inflate and deflate is kicked up a notch. Breathing not only speeds up but also becomes shallower. On the other hand, if you are aware of your breathing you can become more relaxed by learning to slow down and deepen each breath.

Everyone feels better once they are in control of their breathing, and you can easily learn this by taking a deep sigh, a sigh of relief. Sit down and have a go. Here's how:

1. Take a deep breath in through the nose and then let the air out slowly through the nose. This slow gentle exhale is the key to sigh breathing. Try to make the outward breath as long as possible, as if you were sighing deeply.
2. Got the hang of that? Fantastic. Inhale slowly, counting in your head: one, two, three, four. Pause. Exhale slowly: one two, three, four. Pause. Inhale: one, two, three, four. Pause. Exhale: one, two, three, four. Pause. Do this until you get into a rhythm.
3. Now when you breathe out, relax the muscles in the face, jaw and shoulders.
4. Make sure your teeth are not clenched together.
5. Next let go of tension in your chest and stomach. Let your arms and legs relax. As you blow air out through your nose, you should feel a wave of relaxation flow from the top of your head and all the way down to your feet.
6. As you do this, breathe as slowly and deeply as possible, without tension.
7. Repeat ten times. Yes, really.

When we are unable to find tranquillity within ourselves, it is useless to seek it elsewhere.
FRANCOIS DE LA ROCHEFOUCAULD

Defining idea...

Stress is basically a disconnection from the earth, a forgetting of the breath. Stress is an ignorant state. It believes that everything is an emergency. Nothing is that important. Just lie down.
NATALIE GOLDBERG, American author and teacher of creative writing

Defining idea...

How did it go?

Q **My mum and I tried this relaxation exercise, but it made me feel anxious. Why?**

A *That can happen sometimes. Perhaps you weren't completely sure what to expect or do. Some kids have a difficult time relaxing because they have felt tense for so long that it's hard to know how to 'do' relaxation. Try using a very structured approach like reading through the steps of the breathing exercise together, and doing each one together as well. It might also be that this relaxation technique doesn't suit you; you could try something else like swinging on a swing or enjoying a hot chocolate. That might feel more soothing.*

Q **I've got so much on my mind that I can't relax and concentrate on this breathing awareness stuff. Now what?**

A *Many people find they have some initial difficulty thinking about breathing, as it usually happens without any thought going into it. It's especially hard when you have a lot of other things on your mind but, like learning to swim or ride a bike, relaxation is a skill that takes some work. Try practising at a time when you're calm. When other thoughts turn up in your mind, you could gently tell yourself to put them aside until your breathing awareness is over.*

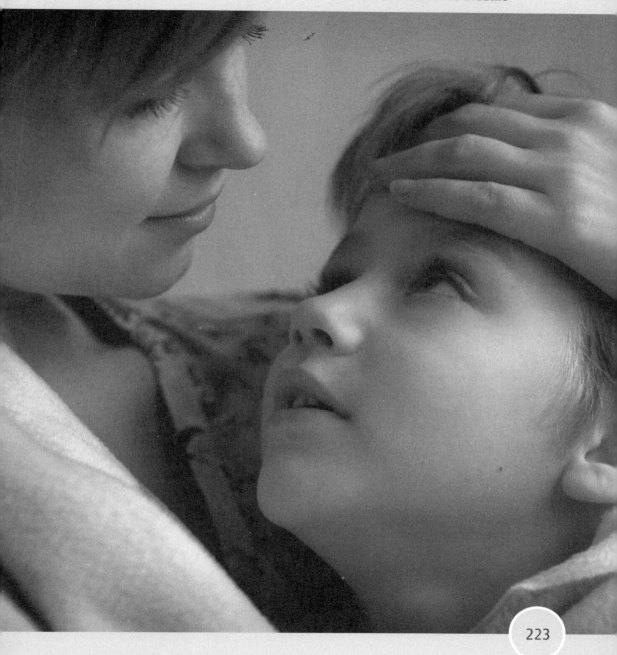

51

Treat yourself

Treating yourself can lessen the effects of bullying. Whether you've had a hard day, or just feel at the end of what you can deal with, it's time for some spoiling.

Finding ways to reward yourself for speaking back to bullies, or even just having endured another day of tormenting, is a great way of getting your self-respect back.

Coping with bullying takes up huge amounts of your understanding, patience and energy. In the middle of it all, it is easy to forget you need to take care of yourself. Let's face it, being at the receiving end of taunts and cruel acts saps your morale like nothing else. What could be better than coming home after a terrible day and soaking in a scented bath until your skin goes wrinkly, then wrapping yourself in a fluffy white towel? For extra decadence, put the towel in the tumble drier before running the bath. Chilling out with a favourite fizzy drink, having an intense gaming session or ignoring the demands of homework for an hour and going to the park and kicking a ball around with some friends are other ways of treating yourself.

Spoiling yourself occasionally is a good way to stay motivated for more bully busting. There will be times when it seems relentless and when it all feels

Here's an idea for you...

Have some me, me, me time and go to the movies at home. Pop some popcorn, snuggle in your favourite chair with your feet up, and watch three upbeat, funny films in a row. Absolutely no weepies.

overwhelming, and that's a good opportunity to indulge in a succession of little treats. Treating yourself has long-term benefits, too. It helps you pick yourself up when the bullies have knocked you down and helps you look forward to a better future.

The fantastic thing about treats is that they can give pleasure well beyond what would seem possible. The secret is to choose the right treats for you. When you're being bullied, it is easy to get swamped in various coping activities and lurch from crisis to crisis, just managing to stay on top of schoolwork and forgetting to enjoy life.

This list might inspire you. Here are some examples of little, inexpensive treats which you could give yourself from time to time if you are being bullied, or you will get ground down and have little energy left for dealing with the bullying. Having a small selection of treats to hand means that there is always a morale booster ready. They needn't be costly, either – it's often the small things that make us feel good – and some of these don't cost anything.

- Stickers
- Bookmarks
- Gel pens
- Bath essences and oils
- Finger puppets
- Stuffed animals
- Plastic or rubber figurines
- Toy cars
- Having a mini manicure

- Making a model kit plane
- Marbles
- Playing cards
- Playing with a pet
- Vegging out in scruffy clothes
- Key rings
- Trendy shoelaces
- Earrings
- Bubble fluid with wand
- Balloons
- Temporary tattoos
- Face masks
- Chocolate
- Candles
- Lollies
- Jazzy nail files

The way you treat yourself sets the standard for others.
SONYA FRIEDMAN, writer

Defining idea...

Being bullied can leave you feeling full of shame and anger, but kind acts towards yourself leave you feeling warm and cared for. People who regularly treat themselves often feel more optimistic and energised about life in general. They tend to be less self-critical and more confident, which are great attributes to have when fending off bullies. Perhaps the best way to treat yourself is with regular doses of kindness, being gentle with yourself instead of harsh or critical when you feel you're not coping at your best, forgiving yourself when you get snappy with someone instead of beating yourself up.

If you must love your neighbour as yourself, it is at least as fair to love yourself as your neighbour.
NICHOLAS DE CHAMFORT, French writer and thinker

Defining idea...

227

It might not come naturally at first. This is because although it sounds simple, treating yourself is quite skilful and like any new or rusty skill it needs to be practised and developed. Give yourself permission to have treats. If you're finding it hard to justify, remind yourself that little treats bring pleasure, and pleasure takes the sting out of bullying.

Finally, when you're kind to yourself, you start being kinder to others too. How about treating someone else who's being bullied?

How did it go?

Q **I've got so much stress, not just bullying but schoolwork too. I'm studying, trying to keep up with the friends I have got, and trying to find ways of coping with bullying on top of all that. How will getting a face mask really help me?**

A *It is when pressures are really biting that treats become especially important. Starting to treat yourself can feel strange when you aren't used to it, particularly if you are feeling stressed. Being kind to yourself isn't the same as being self-indulgent. My advice is to start slowly. Try to give yourself a treat once a week, and work up to having a treat every day while you're going through all these pressures.*

Q **I get bullied, but my sister doesn't. My parents think that if they treat me but not her, they won't hear the end of it. What do you think?**

A *Bullying places serious emotional demands on kids and rewarding them from time to time for their endurance is a good thing. They could ward off sibling rivalry by doing some spoiling things the whole family can enjoy, like having a relaxing weekend away, or a trip to a zoo or park, or an outing for pizza, or going to see a film together...*

52

Forgiven

Forgiving bullies can be one of the most powerful things you do. It's also one of the most challenging ideas to put into practice.

Pardoning bullies might sound like they're getting away with it. But forgiveness reduces anger, stress, painful feelings and restores hope. This is for you, not them.

Grudges are heavy. Forgiveness lightens that load. You're likely to be familiar with amazing stories of forgiveness, like Gandhi forgiving his assassin as he lay dying, the Holocaust survivors who have forgiven their tormentors, the Biblical story of the prodigal son. These stories can be inspiring, but they can also make forgiveness seem like one of those virtues practised by saints in silent monastic orders, rather than by ordinary people in noisy classrooms. Forgiveness can be much more humdrum and routine. But learning to forgive bullies means that you are able to let go of your feelings of anger, resentment and hurt and are able to move forward and get on with a happier future. It's extremely difficult to do, but really, really powerful. It is definitely worth the effort.

One reason why it is difficult to forgive bullies is that anger makes us feel powerful. It makes us feel in control when bullies have left us feeling feeble and powerless. Everyone struggles with forgiveness because when we stop feeling angry, we often

Here's an idea for you...

Don't let the sun go down while you're seething with anger or burning with hurt. Instead of lying awake plotting revenge, try this. Before going to sleep, in your mind acknowledge any resentment, anger, disappointment, frustration and other painful emotions that have arisen. Let go of any destructive emotions that have come up during the day because of bullying.

feel weak and ineffective, completely unable to control anything. Feeling in control of something, even angry or hurt feelings, tricks people into thinking they are in control of the bullying they are undergoing. I say 'tricks', because actually anger and resentment continues to hurt us, so the idea that staying angry means we're staying in control is bunkum. Forgiving puts us in control, but in peaceful, composed control.

Sometimes it might feel that you are being expected to forget what has happened, or pretend bullying never took place, but this isn't the case. Many people misunderstand forgiveness and think that this is making excuses for bullies, or letting them off the hook. Nothing could be further from the truth. Clemency doesn't mean bullies are not accountable for their appalling behaviour, nor that they can't be taught to put things right when they have done something wrong. Bullies can be taught how to make amends, but this is separate from the act of pardoning them, which allows you to move on and not be ground down by an ever-increasing list of wrongdoing.

Dr Robert Enright, an educational psychologist at the University of Wisconsin-Madison who founded the International Forgiveness Institute, has led a number of groundbreaking studies into forgiveness. He emphasises that forgiveness is not forgetting, excusing or condoning, reconciling or weakness. Rather, forgiveness means choosing to stop feeling angry, hurt or resentful, or seeking revenge. And people who forgive have better physical and mental health than those who bear grudges. The good news is that you don't have to be a Catholic nun or a Buddhist monk to forgive. You don't even have to be religious.

Forgive your enemies, but never forget their names.
JOHN F. KENNEDY

Defining idea...

Try these five steps to forgiveness:

1. Understand that forgiveness is for your benefit and not for the benefit of the bullies.
2. Be aware that by forgiving, you are taking an important step towards healing your own wounds and sad feelings.
3. Think hard about what happened and reflect on the events. Make a list of all the actions you need to forgive.
4. Think about how they have made you feel. Some people find it helpful to write this down.
5. Decide to forgive, realising that forgiveness sets you free from harmful emotions. If you have made a list, you might like to tear it up. As you do this, let the anger and pain go, and welcome positive emotions in their place.

It can feel overwhelming to do all this, especially when you are new to the concept of forgiving bullies. Recognise that trying any of the above steps is, in itself, a good achievement and work down the list at your own pace. It is important to forgive in your own time and when you feel ready. Forgiving before you feel fully able to do so can be harmful as it can backfire, leaving you feeling bad about yourself, rather than hopeful. The most important step is making the decision to forgive.

To err is human; to forgive, divine
ALEXANDER POPE

Defining idea...

231

How did it go?

Q   **I can get with the idea of forgiving the bullies, but I don't want to tell them I forgive them in case they think they can just carry on being mean. What do you suggest?**

A   *You don't have to tell anyone you forgive them. Forgiveness happens in your own head and heart. Forgiveness is important for you, as it will help you heal inside, but it is not important for the bullies to know that you forgive them.*

Q   **The bullies have never apologised to me. Don't people have to ask for forgiveness?**

A   *Ideally yes, but they often do not. If you wait for an apology before forgiving, you could be waiting for a very long time. If it never comes, and you are unable to forgive without one, you remain a victim rather than being free to move on with your life. Holding on to resentments is more detrimental to you than it is to any bully.*

The end...

Or is it a new beginning?

We hope that these ideas will have helped you banish the bullies for good. Whether you're a parent, a teacher or a bullied child, using a handful of the ideas in this book should really have helped in tackling the taunts and combating the physical side of bullying.

So why not let us know about it? Tell us how you got on. What did it for you – which ideas really sent the tormentors packing? Maybe you've got some tips of your own that you'd like to share. And if you liked this book you may find we have even more brilliant ideas that could help change other areas of your life for the better.

You'll find the Infinite Ideas crew waiting for you online at www.infideas.com.

Or if you prefer to write, then send your letters to:
Bullying
Infinite Ideas Ltd
36 St Giles, Oxford, OX1 3LD, United Kingdom

We want to know what you think, because we're all working on making our lives better too. Give us your feedback and you could win a copy of another **52 Brilliant Ideas** book of your choice. Or maybe get a crack at writing your own.

Good luck. Be brilliant.

Offer one

CASH IN YOUR IDEAS

We hope you enjoy this book. We hope it inspires, amuses, educates and entertains you. But we don't assume that you're a novice, or that this is the first book that you've bought on the subject. You've got ideas of your own. Maybe our author has missed an idea that you use successfully. If so, why not send it to yourauthormissedatrick@infideas.com, and if we like it we'll post it on our bulletin board. Better still, if your idea makes it into print we'll send you four books of your choice or the cash equivalent. You'll be fully credited so that everyone knows you've had another Brilliant Idea.

Offer two

HOW COULD YOU REFUSE?

Amazing discounts on bulk quantities of Infinite Ideas books are available to corporations, professional associations and other organisations.

For details call us on:
+44 (0)1865 514888
Fax: +44 (0)1865 514777
or e-mail: info@infideas.com

Where it's at...